BABY,
I'M THE BOSS
OF ME

ALSO BY RUTH YUNKER

Me, Myself and Paris

Paris, I've Grown Accustomed To Your Ways

BABY, I'M THE BOSS OF ME

EMBRACING THE POWER AND JOY OF GETTING OLDER

RUTH YUNKER

AUTHOR OF *ME, MYSELF AND PARIS*

COVER ILLUSTRATION BY GINGER TRIPLETT

outskirts
press

Use Your QR App
To Learn More Today

For my wonderful children Joshua and Dana
Through you I learned the meaning of unconditional love

Table of Contents

BABY,
I'M THE BOSS
OF ME

Veering on Vintage?

I am a writer, a traveler, a photographer. I'm a Baby Boomer yoga person, a cashew lover, a crossword puzzle solver. I am a mother. I'm a cat lover and I want a dog. I have a new car. I save wrapping paper.

I am middle aged...

Middle aged?

I cringe at those words, oh yes I do, because what I really am, what I will always be deep inside, is a wide-eyed, know-it-all superwoman, defiantly believing in ironic fairy-tales and realistic possibilities.

The middle aged thing doesn't work. Not at all...

But unfortunately, the fact is, I *am* middle aged. I'm a new kind of middle aged to be sure, the New Millennium middle aged superwoman, but...well, you know...

This means, of course, I'm traveling with lightening speed down that inevitable road to, I whisper, old age.

I'm veering on vintage, I whisper, to lighten the mood.

Of course, maybe I'm simply veering?

That scoliosis and all?

Maybe I'm simply tilting in the wind.

Maybe tilting *with* the wind?

So much more organic.

But whatever.
Here I am now—
And I've been wondering, hoping, praying—
That there are alternatives to this getting old thing...other than actually doing so.
Please make there be alternatives—
Gold paved alternatives.
Happy, fun, fluffy alternatives.
Powerful alternatives, too.
But—
"No, darling, no," I hear myself whisper.
"There's only one way,
"If one keeps on living.
"One gets old."
Including me.

We were in the car going to my older brother's birthday dinner. I was staring out the window at small airplanes parked at the Santa Monica Airport, minding my own business.

All of a sudden, presaged by an insistent whistle in my ears, my brain swept into a shrieking melt down. A claustrophobic swamp of heat burst into my core as I realized with searing horror that one day I would be old. I would be very very old. I would be elderly, wheel-chair bound, wrinkled, weak, decrepit and miserable. This realization burst like a flaming spike through my psyche, there in the backseat of the car on the way to dinner at an elegant restaurant. I went cold with terror. I saw a fractured reflection of my face in the window staring back at me, mindless holes where my eyes should have been.

I don't know where this attack came from. I had never given old age a thought. My parents were only in their forties. I didn't really know my grandparents—

The blinding fear and panic lasted for no more than a minute. I was an optimistic, and in fact arrogant, nineteen year old, just about to burst forth into my very own newly blooming adulthood. I was self-protective and not given to melt-downs. I was not going to let my over-active imagination drag me down into any pointless pit. Automatically I drew in a sharp breath, rapped my brain and heart with cold-blooded knuckles and whispered, "Later I'll be old. But I'm not now. Not even close." My breath slowly calmed down. "I'm nineteen," I assured the black holes in the car window popping wildly at me. "Only nineteen. I'm not going to be old for a long time."

That was many many many...okay, enough...years ago.
Old age is now not far far away.
Old age is near. Old age is hovering like the mosquito waiting for the lights to go out so it can attack my warm body with belligerent accuracy.
Yes, old age is hovering.
But, and this is a fat and juicy but—
Having lived this long, with the accrued experiences of life, and some basic fatigue, the brutal fact of my incipient old age has become less intimidating. Its power to scare me is fading.
I still fret. I still wish it weren't so. I think fifty-two would be a good age to be...forever.
But—
I am feeling a certain mature power. A certain mature joy.
I feel wisdom hovering.
I can access laughter and happiness almost with the snap of my fingers.

I am feeling accomplishment. I am at ease in my body, my aching body, but who's counting.

These are good. Therefore, at this point in my life, I plan to consciously nurture the wisdom, the joy, the accomplishment and the power, that is creeping in.

Because there is no other way to go.

My life's path is now aimed straight at old age. Nothing I can do about it.

I'm here because I've managed to live this long. And now the impulse, the emotion that roars in, the intense sense of promise that flows in flooding my being, is one of excitement. Excitement because I'm planning to live this new and last phase of my life with both power and calm conviction.

And humor. I never forget humor. My favorite, humor.

One day, two years ago, I decided to give up the bad habit of thinking worry, panic and rage were justifiable and indeed, empowering.

I knew about giving up bad habits. For instance, alcohol. I quit alcohol at the turn of the century, and lived to find happiness. Who knew?

I gave up fear of moving to a new place, in other words fear of huge change, fear of being a stranger in a strange land, at twelve, when we moved from California to Belgium and I was thrust into a foreign land and had to learn a new language just to buy a movie magazine.

I gave up fear of losing my freedom and youth when my first child was born. Because I found a new freedom in the maturity motherhood brought me.

So I decided to give up worry, panic and rage. I knew it wouldn't happen overnight. I knew there would be backsliding. I knew it would take practice and patience to get to the other side.

But I knew, in the end, the changes would be magnificent.

So I have given up worrying, panic and rage about getting old. And I'm getting pretty good at it.

Don't get me wrong. There's a lot to complain about. A lot.

I'm not a little sweetheart. I'm not wearing rose-colored glasses. I nurture a certain cynicism that I like to think keeps me from flying off to fairyland wearing the wrong shoes.

I don't love the reality that I am getting older. But the bald-faced truth is, I am. Seemingly more rapidly than I ever could have imagined back there in that car by the Santa Monica Airport with my family, age nineteen.

But since I can't worry about it, or fret or get pissed off or rage or cry or quit, I'm going to look at it as a wondrous challenge.

Because, baby, I am the boss of me.

In my life, as in yours, there are stories of all kinds. These stories comprise this book.

There are my memories. I was a perennial New Kid. My parents were Southerners in a New England world. I lived in Europe at a time when what I wanted most was to be a normal American teenager like Ann-Margaret in Bye Bye Birdie.

There are motherhood stories. Feeding the new baby. Burying the family kitty. The time Santa Claus was called into question.

There are stories about the minutiae of daily life—the importance of peanut butter sandwiches and a plea for the abolishment of homemade lemonade stands run by confused five year olds.

And most important, there are stories about how I am tackling this aging thing. How I'm attempting to get some Attitude to carry me through. Like the day I discovered my eyebrows had let me down. Like the day I told my beloved but disapproving daughter about the facelift. Like beginning to see how perfectly beautiful the truly elderly women in my life still are. How vibrant and powerful.

So much of my life was unplanned. But now that I'm here, on the blithering cusp of old age, well, that just won't do.

So am I a man or a mouse? Am I a kitten or a tiger? Am I a lemming or the one and only boss of me?

I am the one and only boss of me.

Now I'm taking care to greet these last years with as much power and humor and yes well, common sense…as I can muster—

Because the more I pay attention to this time of my life, the more I realize it is developing into an amazing journey—

If I take it in stride.

If I insist I laugh.

If I embrace this older, wiser, more pulled together me.

Because who wants to get old?

Not me.

But since I am, quite vigorously it seems,

Here is how the situation looks to me.

The Little Smile

One day, out of nowhere, literally nowhere, an innocent glance in the mirror, and a chasm cracks open. There they are. The Jowls. Attached with appalling precision to our formerly pristine faces. They are newly minted. Fresh as strawberries in spring. Jowls so miniscule no one else notices them. But we do. Oh, my yes, we definitely do.

Age has come. There's nowhere to run.
Dark angels roar in.
Our psyches crash.
Our personal charisma disappears.
Death looms-
And there's nowhere to hide.
May I lean carefully against this wall now.

It was when I was in my forties and living in Ponte Vedra, Florida, a place where women paid serious attention to their looks, I first noticed the phenomena in which women of a certain age wore tentative little smiles as they hastened into the grocery store. At the time I attributed this to an even temperament, a certain innate kindness, and the joy at getting out of the Floridian heat and into air-conditioning.

But looking back, I realize, no. That little smile had nothing to do with the heat.

And everything to do with an ill-considered attempt to hold up The Jowls.

This state of affairs occurs at a different time for everyone. But you'll know its happened when you find yourself affecting a tremulous little smile the minute you are out of your car and coming in contact with anyone under the age of thirty-five. The kid who bags your groceries. The gum-chewing punk who waits with ruthless politesse while you fumble in your purse for correct change. When the harried mom bursts in front of you in line with barely an apology because she's busy playing Supreme Boss every day.

That little smile begins to occur automatically.

Okay, listen up:

That little smile does not hold up jowls.

Instead, it makes us look timid, self-effacing, and scared of dogs. Do not walk around with that tentative little smile. This vaguely pleasant smirk on the face makes nothing look better. Trust me.

The little smile, also known as pathetically eager-to-please, is not my style. (Nor is it yours, I'm dead certain). So I've hunted down other methods to erase my age from public view. I'm not talking plastic surgery here. More about that later. I'm pro plastic surgery, don't you worry.

I'm also not talking about peace, serenity, or inner acceptance either. More about that later, as well.

I'm talking Attitude and um…getting some.

This Attitude is not street punk or any other age-inappropriate behavior. Of course not. This Attitude is all about maintaining face with dignity, elegance and vivacity while tiptoeing into those elderly years we see looming so vividly.

I dream of emulating the Tough Dame who's seen and done it all, or the Self-made Billionaire who wears her personal toadies like minks wrapped around her shoulders, or the Athlete whose body seems to yield nothing to the aging process, the Diva who believes she still looks as she always has, or even the Saint who pretends she doesn't care, because she pretends she hasn't noticed her jowls, is never going to notice her jowls, and if you mention that word in her presence, she'll spit in your face.

However my inner coward can only take on so much. So while the above are star-quality and gold-plated, I'm opting for a kind of middle-of-the-road Self-made Billionaire Dame Diva Athlete Saint.

One must start their new Attitude somewhere.

I have started mine small, at one of my favorite bêtenoirs. The grocery store check-out line. This is where, in my cold-hearted youth, I abhorred the old cronies, male or female, who held up the proceedings time and time again because age had apparently destroyed their ability to do anything efficiently. As one elderly after the other had a crisis in the check-out line at the grocery store, I wanted to mow them down. Instead, I vowed to never be like them.

Hence, when I needed a New Attitude for the great big world that disdains the older persons inhabiting it, conducting myself at the grocery store line like the hyper-efficient control freak I used to be, is where I started.

I have become a Type A, OCD in the grocery store check-out line. I am organized and pulled together to the max, my items arranged on the counter in a way that screams manic control issues. Most importantly, I do not, *under any circumstances*, wait until *after* my food has been tallied and bagged to begin the search for the check book or wallet. This allows me to forgo the low mewling that goes on all the while the jowl-ridden elderly hopelessly searches for any accoutrement he/she may have in her purse/jacket pocket related to the pressing issue of paying.

I'm on it. I am so on it.

To that end, I don't do change. I don't hunt for quarters, dimes, nickels or pennies. Ever. "No," I say politely, "I don't have a nickel or $.37 or even so much as a penny." I ignore the existence of change in the check-out line at the grocery store. I hand over bills, take what change I get, and dump it into my purse as quickly as possible. My real OCD inner self cringes about ever finding it again. But the outer Billionaire Dame Athlete Diva Saint holds her head high, flashing a blinding smile at the check-out person. She then departs quickly and efficiently, leaving the next person in the grocery store check-out line regarding her with admiration…and okay, if not that, at least sighing with relief the bumbling old woman in front of him wasn't a bumbling old woman after all.

It's when I get home that I have the existential crisis retrieving all the change from the depths of my cavernous purse. Which I then deposit into a Tupperware container where I can ignore its very existence forever. Because as much as change accumulates amazingly in my purse, it takes years to fill a good size Tupperware container. And I mean the size big enough for bringing sliced fruit to a pot luck. Not the small size one used for grated cheese or pickled ginger.

So see? I'm talking about how we comport ourselves out in public after a certain age, after those little jowls have appeared and shaken us to our core.

Quick fixes as opposed to behavioral ones include wearing big sunglasses. Jackie Kennedy did. We all remember her, don't we?

Wear lipstick. I had to be dragged kicking and screaming to that cliff. And now I wonder why. Wear red lipstick.

Leave the smile at home. Absolutely not a glimmer of a smile. Think back to when we were the disaffected young things. Think Julie Christie in 'Darling', Cher when she was Sonny and Cher, Ali McGraw before yoga and too much sun. We had that look of world weary disdain down flat. It wasn't faked either. Remember that? Get some of that back, even if inside you are all sunny and happy. It won't affect the sunny and happy. The sunny and happy inner you will rejoice at the respect the unsmiling (but not angry) face elicits.

Another Attitude changer to consider? The hair.

Our shining glory. Our personal statement. Our very own hair.

Some women have gorgeous heads of hair that spring effortlessly from their head, bountiful, so bountiful it doesn't matter what color it is. I try not to hate these women, particularly if they are my age. With their hair, they never have to worry. Right?

"Oh yeah?" says one of my oldest friends who has an unbelievably magnificent mane of hair. "I hate washing my hair. It takes forever. Combing it out is a nightmare. When I pull it back, my ponytail is so heavy I get a headache. The upkeep for color is astronomical." I look at her and try and try to emphasize, because she is, after all, in one of my favorite age groups—mine. But I just don't feel her pain. She tosses her head of major hair, and says "Okay. Fine." And the subject is closed.

I don't have a lot of hair, but it's very very blonde. I'm happy about that, because it's not how I began life. I was a brunette. Indeed, I *am* a brunette. Although according to my hairdresser I'm now almost white, underneath. "Almost," he says with a hopeful glint in his eyes. "There are amazing shades and variations of white out there. And buzz cuts, while we're on the subject of attitude, go get some," he says.

"Forget it," I rasp out. "I'm not over the Jowls," I whisper.

"What jowls," he says. Good man, my hairdresser.

I did not seek out blondness. It was not part of a plan to keep me on top of the age thing. But that is exactly what it turned out to be.

I'd just moved back to California. I had been streaking my hair to cover the grey. And having it cut shorter and shorter, but not too short. I was being reasonably in acceptance that my hair was a shadow of its former self…I thought.

I walked into a brand new hairdresser. I will not go into the terror of the new hairdresser issue, but you know what I'm talking about. I told him I wanted more of the same. More streaks to cover the grey, and neaten up that nondescript cut.

He didn't waste a minute. "Why don't you just do it?" he said.

"Do what," I said, sensing danger.

"Go blonde. Go platinum blonde. Go for it." I gaped at him. My whole identity was mortally threatened. I was a brown haired girl. Ballet buns and I were one. As were pearls. Trench coats, belted, with a nice scarf. Bleached blonde was so not me. Couldn't he see that?

I didn't know where to look. But then I glanced at myself in the mirror. I saw a woman who didn't look particularly brunette, whose hair hadn't been long enough to pull back into that sleek bun for years, who, in fact, looked nothing like the woman I fondly remembered from a decade ago. I saw a woman vaguely resembling me who had a nowhere cut and those weird streaks looking like a woman who would also outline her lips way outside their natural line, except she was scared of lipstick.

He stood there, behind the chair, dark eyes staring me down.

I'd just turned fifty. I was still in awe of that fact, and not in a good way. I'd been cut off at the knees. Why hadn't my mother warned me?

And now right here, right now, this guy, this stranger was throwing me a road never remotely considered. I wavered—

"But it will ruin my hair."

"No no! We don't even actually bleach your hair."

"But um…I'll look like an idiot. I don't want to look like an idiot."

"You'll look incredible," he said with such confidence I remembered why we love our hairdressers. And then he shut up and waited. One of my husbands told me that once you've made the sale, close your mouth and wait. That's what this guy did.

I wavered. To be or not to be a blonde?

A blonde? Me? I'm a brunette. I'm a serious person. Nobody takes dyed blondes seriously…

What will my friends say? Even worse, what will my children say?

This is ridiculous. I'm not going blonde. It's not me.

But who are you, I asked the shaky version of the woman I thought I used to be, hovering nervously in the mirror…

And the little cherry-flavored devil on my shoulder

whispered in my ear, "Where's your courage, woman?" He bit my neck. It hurt. "Get some, now!"

I…wobbled to the occasion.

"Okay," I said, head sort of held high. Chin sort of jutting out, I'm sure. I went cold, and saw a white light, so I couldn't see the head held high and the chin…well you know what I mean. "Okay do it."

"I'll give you a new cut too."

And whisked away before I could say "Wait. What?"

Five million hours later I emerged, blonde and beautiful, new cut and all, and I've never looked back.

That drastic change of color gave me a shove like I've never had before. Right into the oncoming dreaded older years. It gave me a new persona to try on, to develop in spite of myself, to see who she was, who she was going to be.

If this is a route that has a certain appeal, then go for it. Jump. And remember, it doesn't matter what color you pick.

After my mother's death, my father attended a grief group. One woman wore a purple wig. "I've always wanted purple hair," she said. "So if not now, then when?" and smiled through her tears.

I have another friend who went from brunette to mahogany red. Oh the glory of that red hair! She was sixty-five, and she too never looked back.

And of course all those blondes you see…let me just say, it's an easy switch from gray to blonde. Not hard on the hair at all.

But oh the morale?

Fireworks!

The other day, as I was slumping into the grocery store, I was passed by an elegant eighty-something woman briskly hastening in. She was beautifully dressed, her platinum white hair the work of a gifted hairdresser, make-up was perfection, and as she swept by a light whiff of her perfume enveloped me. It was glorious and I fell in love. I rushed up to her. "Excuse me," I said. "Your perfume is fabulous!" In spite of myself, I half expected her to fall on her face with pleasure at being complimented.

Her fine dark eyes glanced sharply up at me, taking in my windy adoration. "Boucheron, darling," she said, her voice a velvet growl. "Boucheron. I've been wearing it for years." And then she gone, lost in the aisles of my local grocery store.

There had not been a glimmer of a little smile.

The New Kid

"Boys and girls? Pay attention. Look up here. Right next to me. See this huddled mass of misery? She's the New Kid. Every one of you is going to be her new friend. Okay? Because believe me, she needs friends. This new kid has no friends. Okay, maybe she had some back wherever she came from, but we don't care about that, do we? No. We only care about our world here, where this person thinks she has a prayer of happiness. Which she does. Right, boys and girls?"

I'm eleven years old, and whereas the moment before when I slunk through the door of this new classroom, I was tall for my age, I am now two inches high. I'm not looking at the faces staring at me like hungry sharks. I am staring at the floor, and thinking through what would happen if I ran hysterically from the room—

Because this isn't the first time I have been caught like a rat in this horror show. I ran that time back in second grade, newly arrived at St. Joe's grammar school, in downtown Pittsfield, MA, from St. John's in Peabody, Massachusetts. Eastern Massachusetts and Western Massachusetts—might have been on opposite sides of the planet. That time, back when I was seven, I knew running would only prolong the agony, but I did it anyway.

I was standing in this exact position, up in front of the class, with the nun's arm wrapped around me. I'm sure she felt she was comforting me, since I was seven, not the exalted age of eleven I was now. She was letting me know that while she wasn't my mother, she might somehow be channeling my mother's love. Forget it, honey. Tears began to fall. I had to run, and so made a break for the door. But I was caught and immediately hustled off to the principal, Sr. Mother John, where she sat me on her voluminous lap. And then, on cue, one kid from every class in the school came in to deliver their classes' roll for the day. So each and every one got a good look at the tear-stained new kid. That's when I learned not to meet anyone's eyes until I knew I had it together.

"This is Ruth Yonkers," says the nun, now, here in my newest school. Linoleum is the floor here. Last school, the old Catholic school in Pittsfield, MA, had wooden floors. This is a Catholic school too. But it's new. I'm way over on the other side of the country in a place called Oakland. I didn't even know Oakland, CA existed until three months ago. I called my best friend, Andi McCall. "We're moving away," I whispered into the phone. "To Oakland, CA," I said a little louder.

"Where's that?" Andi croaked.

"Who knows," I wailed.

Now here I am. The nightmare has come true. I have moved, and yet once again I am the New Kid. Standing up in front of the class like some side-show, being introduced to a bunch of happy, relaxed, comfortable and established old kids.

"Ruth Yonkers," repeats the teacher. I nod. I just don't care. I have one of those last names people can't be bothered to get right. "Class, I give you the New Kid."

Being the New Kid seven times, including first grade, has made me the self-confident woman I am today, okay? I can go anywhere. Fit in anywhere. Eat anywhere. Win arguments with anyone. I like odd people and get away with it because I also like normal people and they like me.

I know how to dress in different local customs. I know how to joke in different lingos. I know how to laugh at jokes told in foreign accents. I know how to say hi on the phone in any place I end up and sound like a local. I know there's even such a thing as a local. I knew this by seven years old when I found out I wasn't one.

I know how to be friendly too…if the occasion calls for it. Relaxed and easy-going, even while nothing around me is recognizable.

I'm an amateur sociologist. I understand English spoken in a foreign accent (which too many Americans do not). I understand because I became that foreigner once, when I was twelve and my parents moved my five brothers and sisters and I from Oakland, CA to Brussels, Belgium, and we were suddenly living in a land of gray skies, gaufres, pomme frites eaten with mayonnaise out of a newspaper cone, and made to learn French with a Belgian accent.

Parisians are the only ones who now disparage my Belgian accent. I know not to take umbrage. I do, however, care what they think about my choice of attire. So when in Paris, I dress like a Parisian. This is called getting along. This is called being a citizen of the world.

This is called being the New Kid, all grown up.

Now I leap at the chance to move. Living in a new place amazes me every day. I have no fear of living among strangers. I make friends anywhere, which means I have a lot of friends, and harbor no worries I may one day find myself without a friend to my name.

But I got like this by being the new kid who constantly needed a new friend. Otherwise one endured lunch and recess, the one bright light in the otherwise dreary school day, skulking about alone. A miserable state of affairs for anyone, but particularly for the new kid at the new school.

I started young with the new kid business. I started in first grade.

How is this even possible? Even at six I asked myself this. Six is way too early for heavy self-doubt and the role of victim. Six years old is way too early to have to know without a doubt everybody but everybody in your grade is way ahead of you. And that this matters. Oh so very much.

I hadn't gone to kindergarten. There had been no room in the Catholic kindergarten near our house in Peabody, MA. There had been room in the public kindergarten right down the street, but it wasn't Catholic. That didn't cut it with my mother. Nor was I chomping at the bit to get out of the house.

So when I hit first grade, I was newly hatched from the nest. I didn't have the sophistication of having experienced and survived the rigors of kindergarten. I still had Mommy love fuzz all over me.

This is how it felt to me. I felt my Mom had suddenly, and for no good reason, thrown me out of the house. I was shocked to my core. I thought I'd always have a place at home with Mom, but apparently not. Because the day came, one fine Monday morning, when I was dressed up in strange clothes. I was given a plaid lunchbox...I still don't like plaid. I was put on a bus with my twelve-year-old brother, while my younger brother got to stay at home with Mom.

And I was delivered to prison...*two weeks* after the school year had started. Two weeks was a lot of time. Friends had already been made. Habits and patterns learned and routines established.

This painful scenario had happened because my four year old brother contacted a minor case of polio, and we were quarantined. I vaguely remember my older brother being ecstatic about starting school late. Somehow I didn't realize this would impact me. In fact, I really barely realized I was going to go to school. I'm sure my parents told me this, but since I couldn't picture it, I put the whole notion aside.

The first day of school (two weeks late) came. I was wrenched away from my mother, and handed over to the nuns, brought into my first grade classroom, and made to endure the first of the New Kid introductions that were to become the mainstay in my childhood.

I never recovered. Even though I ended up being teacher's pet in first, second and third grade, I simply hated school. Forever. I hate it now, even thinking about it. I'm in a cold sweat writing these words.

I did learn how to make friends, though, like I said.

And I learned there were different accents when one spoke. I learned what accents were...even though my mother never lost her strong southern accent, I had never realized she had one.

The accent lesson happened when we moved from Boston, MA over to Pittsfield, MA, in western Massachusetts in the Berkshires, halfway through second grade. The teacher asked if anyone knew the four sounds of the letter 'a'. I did. But I was new. I was mute. I was alone. However no one raised their hand. So, never one to turn down an opportunity to show how smart I was, I cautiously raised mine. "Ruth," said the teacher, nodding encouragingly. I stood up. I said the four sounds of the vowel 'a' I'd learned in my Boston school. I even made sure I spoke loud enough. Think JFK pronouncing "Ask not what your country can do for you, but what you can do for your country." There was silence. Even the teacher looked stunned.

Then everyone started to laugh. My stomach melted. Teacher came to her senses immediately. "Class," she warned, which terminated the noise. Then to me she said, "Very good. That was correct." I felt a surge of relief, but this lasted only a moment. Teacher went on. "Class," she said. "Ruth has just moved here from Boston. In Boston they speak differently than we do." Now everyone looked surprised. This was weird information for a seven year old. My own brain buzzed with confusion. I'd been having trouble distinguishing the teachers from the students because this was a public school and there were no nuns in their flowing habits, and I didn't like that. But I had certainly been able to understand everyone.

In a state of confusion that night at dinner I told my mother and father. My mother's eyebrows went into her hairline. She looked at my father and said in a voice that had dangerous undertones, "At the public school they don't know their vowel sounds by second grade?"

I was moved to the closest Catholic school a week later where no one laughed at the accent I now knew I had, everyone in my second grade class already knew their vowel sounds, and there were nuns, which I recognized as real teachers. I could sort of breathe again, and go back to simply being the new kid who needed a friend.

I was in sixth grade, five months in from being a New

Kid in Oakland, when my father got the career opportunity of a lifetime in Europe, and without further ado, even after I yelled I hated him, we were transplanted to Brussels, Belgium—

Where three of us (me, younger brother and even younger sister, just starting first grade herself) were sent to the International School of Brussels. The International School of Brussels was an imperious, batting ram of a school, populated by hardened new kids. My older brother stayed in the States, starting college. And the two youngest were still babies sucking their thumbs, not caring where they lived, got to stay at home. I envied them.

This school presented a new, dangerous scenario. I arrived for my first day of school, but received no introduction in front of the class. Nobody cared that I was new. Because so were ninety percent of all the other kids.

This was a school filled to the brim with the military brats, diplomat snobs, entitled corporate kids (this crew included me and my siblings). They were all born and bred New Kids like me. We shared a peripatetic, treacherous school-yard history, making normal relationships impossible.

Since being a New Kid at The International School of Brussels was beside the point, the "old" kids, for once in their painful school careers, lorded it over the place with the clumsiness but strength of a bully made, not born. It was sink or swim.

Not sure how to handle this new gruesomeness, I dog paddled my way through. And it was here that I understood for the first time, it was not necessarily best for me, or even prudent for me, to try and bond, find true love or even a best friend. Because this whole existence would be a moot point in three or so years anyway. And nobody was going to bother to be nice, loyal or fond of me. Not for long anyway, because the next move was only a moment away.

The kids were sophisticated. All were world travelers. Which is what I was becoming. And though in every way we all tried to be as American as possible, there in dark, dreary, but oh so cosmopolitan Brussels, Belgium, it was only upon arriving back in the United States, that I saw how far removed from an actual home grown, one town fits all-American kid who'd never lived anywhere else, we all were. How different I was.

Our passports were beaten up. We spoke more languages than English. We could keep our money straight in francs, lira, kronin. We knew how to fly on transatlantic flights by ourselves. And we all missed being US teenagers down to our bones while wearing European clothes, using European manners like shaking hands with everyone, eating escargot because they were fabulously decadent, and going to Spain for the beach vacation, wishing wishing wishing we were back in the States with real American teenagers in Cape Cod or Colorado or someplace really American like that.

The school itself tried to create a social life with American over tones. We had baseball games. Halloween parties. Weekly school dances with American rock and roll.

But I'd heard kids also had private parties. I wanted to go. I was twelve. I liked boys. I wanted to dance. I wanted to go to a dance party. I wanted to go to a private party.

But it wasn't until my second year there I was finally, *finally* invited to a private party. Okay, so it wasn't an A-list. But it was a list of any kind and somehow I had managed to get on it. I wanted, no I *needed* to go. "Mom," I burst home the day I was invited. Thrilled! "Can I go? Please?!"

My mother checked the dates. "But your father and I are

going to Vienna that week, and we want to bring you with us." Vienna?! She was offering me a gift wrapped in gold—

Okay. There *was* one huge perk to living in Brussels. We got to travel. A lot. To wonderful places. Even better, parents had no compunction about taking the kid out of school for a few days here and there. And the school was okay with it. The unofficial extra-curricular class—International Travel with Parents.

I loved my trips with my parents. I had them, or rather my mother, to myself. I got to miss school. I was a geography lover, and despite of the horror of not getting to be a normal American kid at a crucial time in my life, I loved the traveling, and seeing all the wonderful places I'd studied in geography. Vienna? Are you kidding? The crème de la crème! "There's even a ball. And the opera…" my mother said, but her voice trailed off because I wasn't standing on my head with joy.

Because like…here was a crossroad. Did I choose the glories of Vienna all alone with my parents, while missing school? Or did I choose the b-list party to which I had *finally* been invited, which meant I would now have parties to go to, dancing with boys, and well, hopefully all kinds of thrilling things.

I was better than that…wasn't I?

But…school life loomed too large. It was such a cold place. Here was a step ladder, only three measly rungs though it may be, to a little bit of warmth.

"Mom, I have to go to this party. I just do," I said, painfully bidding farewell to what I knew would have been a glorious trip to Vienna. I actually hung my head.

I know my mother understood. She didn't even take my younger brother, age ten, instead, which she could have done. I suspect he, who was actually thriving at school for the first time in his scholastic career, didn't find the idea of Vienna as enthralling as baseball practice after school. But she never stopped casually throwing tidbits my way about what a glorious trip I had missed. Never.

One day, with the Cuban Missile crisis and Kennedy's assassination propelling my father into action to get his family back to the States, after three years of overseas living and traveling—to Zurich and Geneva, London, Paris, Madrid, Costa Bravo, Lake Como, Rome, Lisbon, Amsterdam, Athens—we prepared to move again.

This move, as if Dad had finally gotten the idea of pleasing his children about a move, he asked my brother and I if we wanted to move to the beautiful Smokey mountains of South Carolina (his choice), or Los Angeles where movie stars lived. Only that's not how he put it. My brother and I, no fools us, chose LA, and sure enough, Dad moved us there, to palm trees, sunshine, the Pacific Ocean, Hollywood Boulevard, gorgeous stores, and a turquoise blue swimming pool in the back yard. I was fifteen, old enough to fall irrevocably in love with our swank new town.

And this also meant I had only three more years of mandatory school.

So, there in Pasadena, California, age fifteen, for the last time I was hauled up in front of the class and introduced. "Class? Class. This is Ruth Yonkers from Brussels, Belgium. She's new here, and in desperate need of friends…"

I was forced to say hello. I didn't cry. I didn't look at the floor. Maybe I even forced a small sneer.

Afterwards one girl sauntered up. "When they told us we were going to get a new kid from Europe, I thought we were getting a real European kid." She checked me up and down. "You're not. You're just American."

I didn't care. What a difference the battle ground at the International School of Brussels had made. I had no fear. Besides, I could see her eyes were friendly. Curious, as opposed to a steely-eyed assessment. I was the one with the steely eyes. "You have a weird accent, at least," she said.

Really? Still? Which one? Southern from Mom? Kennedy from Boston? Flat from Oakland? Euro-infused from my Belgian years?

Was I even still speaking English?

Didn't matter anymore. Three years would fly by.

And this friendly girl with no accent became my seventh, but not least, new best friend.

Secrets Become Lies
in the Eyes of the Beholder

When my daughter was fifteen years old, she found my marijuana. It was buried in my underwear drawer, inside a dark sock, and shoved way to the back. Hidden away but good. She found it anyway. And she was horror-stricken. "You lied to me," she cried. "I asked you if you ever smoked pot. You said no. You lied to me." And then she burst into tears.

I crumbled.

"I didn't tell you because I thought you were too young to understand—" I heard the shaky hope in my voice. I heard the pleading even more.

"You lied to me," she sobbed again. Cautiously I tried to hug her. She backed away from me, furious blue eyes glittering with tears, staring me down.

When I was twelve years old, and my family was living in Brussels, Belgium, one day I figured out my mother and father had been pregnant when they got married nineteen years before. I counted the months between their wedding date and the birth of my older brother, back and forth, back and forth, with growing shock as the truth of it began to glare. It was true. My very own parents. Sex before marriage.

I swept into the warm, steamy, and large European bathroom where baby nightgowns were hanging on the towel warmers, and where my thirty-nine year old mother was on her knees by the huge, soap-filled bathtub, washing two of my little sisters, age three and six. One with a head of black curls. The other strawberry blond curls. The third, an eight-week old baby, was cooing to herself in the background, lying in the bassinet. A lovely, beautiful moment, the air in the bathroom sweet and warm, gentle. Even through my self-righteous shock I could see this was a lovely moment and I shouldn't destroy it. But the door was already open, and puberty-stricken me was there. Betrayed. Heartbroken.

"You *had* to get married!" My voice shook, then broke. I could barely look at my mother. Her beautiful face looked up at me, shock and hideous loss registering simultaneously. "I hate you," I whispered furiously. As I turned to stumble back out of the room before the tears came, I heard one of my little sisters cry out, "Is Ruthie crying?"

Mom came to me after getting my three little sisters to bed. She knocked oh so tentatively on my bedroom door. I was still completely horrified. Completely beaten. But I grudgingly let her in.

She tried to apologize, to explain, especially her own deep regret for what she and Dad had done before they were married. How Dad's mother had made them leave town right after their small wedding and have the baby elsewhere, and how my brother had been three months old when my grandmother finally sent out birth announcements. It had been 1942. The war intervened, but my mother never got over the perceived shame, even though she and Dad went on to have five more children, just to cement the deal.

Later, older and wiser, even before I had a daughter of my own and would then understand even more, I apologized over and over to my mother for that day.

A young daughter's harsh condemnation is unbearable. But we know we aren't liars. We are merely parents, groping our way through.

And later, older and wiser herself, and not the faultless fifteen year old anymore, my daughter told me it wasn't the fact I had smoked pot that hurt her so badly. It was the fact I had lied to her. I had lied when she had been so sure of my trust and faith in her, that I would always tell the truth to her, that we were that perfect mother and daughter.

My lie had held her away. That hurt. That burned.

I wish more than anything I hadn't felt I needed to lie to her about anything, ever.

Smaller mis-directions and straight out mis-directions occur over and over. Some are spur of the moment, when caught off-guard. Some drop out of the sky, even though you suspected the moment of truth would have to occur. As I look back I see them all over the place.

One day my six-year old son rushed in the door from school. I was sitting at the kitchen table drinking coffee with my mother. Joshua slammed his book bag down on the ground and, face red, voice cracking, shouted "Tell me the truth. Is there Santa Claus? Charles told me there's no such thing as Santa Claus, and I bet him all my money that there is too a Santa Claus."

I gaped at him. I'd never made a big deal about Santa Claus. The presents were from me and Grandma and friends and so on. Santa's name was bandied about with fun. Santa Claus was charming. Santa Claus was a fairy-tale.

I'd never said he was real. I simply never said he wasn't real.

But my silence, my not leaping to my feet and calling my son's best friend Charles a liar, told my son the stark truth.

His dark blue eyes grew unbearably wide. His face blotched even more. "Oh no," he wailed. And flew up to his room. The slammed door shook the house. My mother and I gazed at each other mutely.

Later Charles' mother called up apologizing profusely. "Charles' know-it-all cousin was here this weekend and he told Charles, and Charles has been on a rampage ever since." Charles was not allowed to accept my son's life fortune of $78.

"Did you really believe in Santa Claus?' I asked softly, tucking him into bed early that night, he was that wrung out. His little sister, hovering anxiously by the door, also waited for the answer.

There was a silence. Then he whispered "No. But I wanted him to be."

Lies we tell. Half-truths we tell, hoping no one is listening too closely.

And then there are the assertions of truth we are constantly being called on to make which we can't know for sure, but really really hope are not lies-

Lies that can open the way to truth, in spite of themselves.

Our middle cat, Patches, a big ole orange sweetie pie of a tabby, was found dead one morning. He hadn't come in the night before. But there he was that next morning, lying on his side by the garage door, looking like he was asleep.

He was only a year old. My children were eight and six. Our other two cats hovered fretfully as I rushed over to my little guy, tears stuck in my throat. But instantly I took care to be calm for my children. I tried to pretend this was very sad and awful, but that it was also normal. That pets did die. And sometimes pets die young. Not often. Look how old our Poppycat was. But sometimes, yes, too young, like just now.

My children nodded wide-eyed, the experience too new for them to have formed an awareness of the reality. Except that their wonderful kitty was dead. And this was too big to take in. Inside I was throbbing with shock. I'd always known when my animals were sick. But not with Patches. I'd suspected nothing.

"We must bury him," I said. They nodded. We decided to bury him out in the forest alongside the house. "I'll find the shovel," I said. This galvanized Dana and Joshua, and tears now beginning, they ran off. By the time I had wrapped our sweet Patches in a soft crimson towel and put him inside a heavy-duty trash bag and carried him out to the woods, my children had gathered their little band of friends. A pile of bicycles now scattered the driveway.

There was Charles and Amanda. There was Alex and Ian. There was Sami and Chip. There was Meryl and Gabi. All between six years old and ten. They stood there silently, gazing up at me in misery. They all had their own pets. They understood the pain. Gabi held Dana's hand tight. Charles had his arm around Josh's shoulder.

It was a beautiful late spring day. I pushed the shovel into the ground, and said a quick prayer of relief the ground wasn't frozen.

It didn't take much. A small and reasonably deep hole was dug. I looked around for my son. He seemed to have aged ten years. I nodded at the very still bag that held our Patches. He picked it up, and both he and Dana laid it carefully down into the hole, Dana's silent tears dripping onto the black plastic, running down the edges. They straightened up and stepped back into the warm, safe cluster of their friends. I filled the hole back up. Then I paused, unsure how to proceed.

"Mrs. Yunker?" I looked down at the circle of strained faces. It was nine year old Alex.

"Yes?"

His dark eyes gazed up at me. He clutched his fingers. "When they die, do animals go to heaven like people do?" Every pair of their young eyes swung up to look at me with such ferocious hope I almost lost my breath. Did animals go to heaven?

Did this question even need to be asked?

In this little group there were Catholics, Muslims, Jews and Baptists. I had no idea what their parents told them or wanted them to believe. I had a brief flash of irate parent phone calls later if I didn't get it right.

But what was right? At that moment, ten little kids, in shock over one of their pets dying suddenly and too young, being put into a black bag and then into the ground and covered up with dirt—it wasn't right. It shook their brand new worlds. My world shook now too, from their young pain, disbelief, and confusion.

"Mrs. Yunker, do animals go to heaven like we do?" They were all staring up at me. Such beautiful, huge, hopefilled eyes. I stood there, their sage, their fountain of truth. What I said, they would believe.

I made up my mind.

"Yes Alex. All animals go to heaven just like human

beings do." My voice was strong, confident, sure. "They're just like us, aren't they? Animals have eyes and ears like us. They have hearts and they breathe, just like us. They love us as much as we love them. Of course all animals go to heaven. They go straight to heaven."

An explosion of relief swept through that young group. The black cloud that had been hanging over the whole proceedings lifted and dissipated. "Of course animals go to heaven," they crowed. "Of course Patches is in heaven. Of course of course…"

They looked up at me beaming. "Let's get things and make Patches' grave pretty," said Meryl, the oldest one. The sun was coming back out. Of course animals go to heaven. They ran off.

And I thought, standing there, "God, You listening? I better be right."

One time I told a lie on purpose, and I believe it was the right thing to do.

My mother was dying. She knew she was dying subliminally, but never wanted to talk about it. She kept hope that she would recover. Even though she knew she was on hospice at home.

But that was my mother. She was her charming Southern self all the way through, gracious to all visitors until she finally asked us to allow no more. She tried to eat her food until she just didn't care enough to swallow, although she knew it made us happy when she did.

Every morning she sat in the living room in her chair with the Pacific Ocean and wide beach spread out before her, holding the newspaper up, pretending to read, pretending to watch the sand cleaner make it's way up and down the beach until it was right in front of the house, pretending to care the waves were huge that day.

She never choked on a pill.

One day she wanted an extra bowl of strawberry ice cream. I was thrilled, then could have screamed when I realized we were all out, but would butter pecan do? It would, but she quietly didn't eat it.

And one time, Dad showing her his new suit, she said to him "Did you buy that to wear to my funeral?" in her soft Southern drawl, and my father berated himself ever after.

In bed at night, as they lay in bed side by side, just as they had done for fifty-nine years, my father said she never talked about death. Never. So he didn't either.

It was four days before she died. Of course I didn't know it was four days before she would die. She was by now full time in her bedroom. My older brother was there, and he was sitting reading in the bedroom while she slept fitfully.

I came in to check her. "Ruthie," she said softly. I was startled. I'd thought she was asleep. "Ruthie…" I bent over her. She half sat up and clutched my shirt sleeve. "Am I dying?" Her soft Southern accent was a lilt.

At her question my mind immediately tail spun into an agony of grief. "Am I dying?" she repeated. Her blue eyes were open. They weren't clear, but she was staring straight up at me. Asking me to tell her. To tell her what I knew. She trusted me. I was her oldest daughter. She would trust my answer.

I looked down at her and in a flash knew what I would say. I knew what she wanted to hear. And since she wanted to hear it, I would say it.

"No Mom," I said quietly. I felt rather than saw my brother lean forward. "You are not dying." But my mother was no fool. So she still clutched my sleeve. "You're not dying right now," I said. "But, you *are* very very sick."

Her face relaxed. She let go of my sleeve. I put my hands under her frail shoulders and laid her back into the pillows. "Yes, I know I'm very sick—" Her eyes closed, and she sank back into sleep.

I didn't promise her she was going to get better. I put one small phrase in there so that if she wanted to hear it, she could. But if I'd bluntly said yes, you are dying, where could she have gone with that? Already confused and in discomfort if not actual pain, already not talking about death at all, what kind of nightmare would I have sent her on for what turned out to be her last few days.

I never told you because—
"I didn't want to hurt you."
"I didn't think you were old enough to understand."
"I didn't know how to."
"I was afraid."
"Because I love you-"

I have a menagerie of folk art animals, and a few mannequins thrown in there for good luck, and they may as well be living breathing members of my household, because that is what they are to me.

Nobody has felt the need to set me straight.

I know my car can't hear me when I talk…because I don't talk loud enough.

I have gotten over needing to believe everything politicians say.

I know my grown kids don't always tell me everything because I wouldn't… understand.

I know my mother helps me, listens to me and answers me. From heaven. Where Patches is too.

Frankly I don't understand how any kid can ever believe in Santa Claus. That's a story that is so implausible it makes Goldilocks read like scientific data. I don't know if I admire or despise the parents who try to preserve the myth for their kids until that heart-wrenching day when they *find out*.

It seems cruel, but I still persist in getting pets whom I know will die and break my heart, break my children's heart. But I wouldn't want to miss out of the love.

Like Santa's love.

Like my mother who had to get married back in 1943 and didn't tell me because she thought I was too young to understand, and she was right.

Years later I found out my daughter smoked. She'd hidden that from me. I'd never suspected. When I found out I was too old to have that kind of melt-down. But it shook me. I wanted to kill her...

"Your grandmother died of lung cancer. What are you doing?"

"Why didn't you tell me?"

Dana called weeks later. "I was driving and smoking. And talking to Meemaw," she said. "I told her I was going to give up smoking very soon. I asked her if that was okay?" There was a pause. "Meemaw seemed kind of quiet," said my daughter. "So I promised her I'd quite smoking very soon. Then, Mom, I flicked my cigarette out the window." I swallowed my instinct to scold. My daughter barely paused. "I was wearing shorts. And Mom, that cigarette came flying back in like it had been shot from a gun, landed right on my bare leg and burned the heck out of it."

My Mom! Thank you.

"You shouldn't have said 'soon'," I said to Dana. "Unless you really meant it."

Another pause. "I do now," my mother's granddaughter said quietly.

White Eyebrows

It's the little things, baby. It's the little things that get you in the end.

It was an innocent night in May. The air was sweet, the sunset ruby red and sapphire, and the cat was purring in the sink.

I was in my bathroom, wearing my favorite pajamas. The ones with the pink cabbage roses. They were ripped and threadbare. But loved. Oh so very loved. My hair looked fabulous, which was a bit of a waste because I was about to go to bed alone. The cat purred louder. Okay, not alone.

So I was in the bathroom, innocently minding my business, when in the mirror I noticed…

Something was not right.

Not a good moment.

It took a full minute to zero in on the issue. And then there it was—

My eyebrows.

Or lack thereof.

Where once I had eyebrows dark enough for me to see without my glasses…now?

I leaned closer.

They had disappeared. My eyebrows had disappeared off my face.

Fury burst forth. No friggin' eyebrows?

This was outrageous! Eyebrows were like noses—here to grow and grow no matter what…weren't they? What about those old Victorian geezers with eyebrows so ferocious they needed to be shorn with a shears? I thought eyebrows stayed put. I thought eyebrows were like Everest. I thought eyebrows were immortal.

Fact was, I had never thought about my eyebrows at all except as having been placed on my face with a lifetime guarantee.

I already knew about disappearing body hair, here, there and everywhere, but flat out on my face with nowhere to hide?

I was speechless with outrage. I'd been good to my eyebrows, unlike say, my knees. I respected their unruliness. Not for me tweezing them into Jean Harlow pencil brows. Audrey Hepburn's luxuriant eyebrows were more my style. Even now they were in the care of an expert eyebrow person who tinted them just enough to add that dash of vivacity to them. So that while not quite Audrey Hepburn anymore, my aging eyebrows held their own in the real world.

I leaned closer to the mirror, my flannel cabbage roses shrinking back. I leaned in so close my nose touched the ice cold, the unforgiving, the all-truthful mirror.

How could they have just disappeared, vanished, since the last visit to my eyebrow person?

And that's when my brain did a second spin of disbelief. This was when my brain, also known here as my psyche, was dealt yet another blow. Because, what I saw, what my brain was trying to put into images my precariously aging psyche could accept without a total collapse, what I saw as clearly as a full moon on a cloudless night, was not thinning eyebrows, not balding brows. Oh no.

What I saw were *white* eyebrows.

My eyebrows hadn't gone bald. They'd gone white. Hot steam formed in my nostrils.

My eyebrows had caved in, bitten the dust, gone organic, and turned white. White as newly laminated teeth, freshly fallen snow, a baby's first tooth...you get the idea.

The stark truth shone like a traffic cop's flashlight in my face. My eyebrows, the dark eyebrows I had known and loved for a whole lot of years, behind my back with nary a warning, had taken the train to old age. They'd laid down their guns. They'd staggered. They'd quit. They'd rolled over and died—

I could have wept. If there had been a ledge, I would have used it. The cat, sensing despair in Paradise, shrank back. The cabbage roses faded still further, in alliance with my yellow bellied eyebrows.

I hated them. Every last traitorous one of them. There in that quiet bathroom, the kitty in the sink, now on alert and no longer purring, I wanted to murder every single whiter than white eyebrow I still had.

It would have been better, somehow, if they had simply disappeared. But they were doing that too, slowly but surely, weren't they?

This was the last straw, okay? I mean the very last straw.

I tiptoed out of the bathroom, and into my bed. I needed a moment, here. I needed a desperate little moment—

The list of pointless aging indignities is long, and getting longer.

There was that day I noticed my elbows had sagged. How come none of the old women who have found aging so enlightening and delightful, ever brought up their sagging elbows. Oh. I know why. They are those delightfully unself-conscious women who just never ever noticed. The delightful aging hippie who graduates from the ripped jeans to flowing muu muus without a fight. Blissfully oblivious.

Well I sure notice. Oh yes I notice! I started noticing aging issues when I was nineteen. But back then, though, I was able to reassure myself I had a long way to go before I really had to worry about getting old. And at nineteen, that was a reasonable assumption to make. I hadn't even had children yet. I had no idea, at nineteen, what was in store.

But eventually, as in all long-lived lives (by that I mean making it to fifty-three, which is the beginning of the end) there came the day when little things, here and there, began to fall apart.

There was the first time I merely turned around to look out the back of the car and threw out my hip.

And the day I first realized I no longer owned a bathing suit. And then, with a small shock, realized I was actually afraid to put one on.

Or the day the cop pulled me over and I saw that he was at least ten years younger than my son.

The day I calculated that if I got a new kitten I would easily be in my eighties before the little thing died.

Eighty years old? It doesn't compute, okay?

But I am there. I am finally at the age when that kind of computation occurs over and over.

That my sister-in-law and I have known each other for fifty years.

That my best friend and I have known each other for thirty-five years.

That my own children are well into their thirties.

That I actually look forward to my social security check.

That Medicare now seems like a Christmas present, so reduced are my monthly insurance payments.

That one day my toenails will be huge, yellow, curled and cracked, and need a garden shears to trim.

That my voice will shrivel, while my nose will continue to grow and grow.

That those are floaters in my eyes, not thousands of insane gnats fluttering around my head.

That I no longer climb straight up on the kitchen counter, fearless and powerful, pulling down the vase from the highest shelf. No. Nowadays I climb up carefully, hugging the cabinets like a baby Panda to its mother.

And that one day I won't even do that.

Okay, so this is the part where I announce that through meditation, yoga, organic goji berries, fasting and regular colonics, deep tissue massages and a mother-lode of money, living in a glamorous place with lots of beautiful clothes and beautiful friends, children with advanced degrees, a hairdresser, facialist, masseuse, Botox person, plastic surgeon, personal trainer—all of whom I adore and give Christmas presents to—an amazing media room, elaborate library and collection of gorgeous orchids I grow from babies, a handsome, age-appropriate man stashed in either my bedroom or his personal jet, I am finally at peace with aging...

Well, I'm made of dreams. Some are realized (the children, friends and plastic surgeon), some partially realized (library, facialist and clothes), and some not realized yet because maybe I don't need them anyway (colonics and a man with a private jet), I am truly okay with...however the hell old I am.

My cat, blue-eyed and Siamese, gave me a moment before joining me on the bed. Then she sat at the edge of the bed, just looking at me. I looked back at her. She wasn't a cat for engaging in a lot of eye contact, but right now she was.

She was an old girl. Her whiskers had gone white. I'd noticed that a few weeks earlier. In her youth an amazingly agile cat, I had recently had to help her down from a tall bookcase from which she used to leap like Superwoman. She didn't really like her food anymore, although she was still up for her nightly treat of whipped cream. She had bad ears, the beginnings of kidney failure, and I was facing the fact we were nearer rather than farther from the day I would lose her.

Of this she was unaware. Blissfully unaware. To her, she was just herself, at one with wherever, whoever and whatever she was now. She sat there gazing at me, waiting until she felt sure I would be settled enough for her to get a good night sleep. She saw the same old me she loved, not a newly aged old woman with white eyebrows. I saw the same old beautiful her I loved. "I want to be just like you," I whispered.

I patted beside me. She came over, a little more stiffly than her youthful leap had been. She settled down, right in her spot by my right hip. Amazing how this little cat became as heavy as a boulder in bed.

She began to purr. I soaked in that wonderful sound. I felt that calming rumble.

White eyebrows? Get over it.

Or try to, anyway.

The Day My Childhood Died

My childhood died the day I got my first bra.

Some idiot girls celebrate that day. I did not. Childhood was good place to be and I knew it. No responsibility, no hard work, no accountability. Childhood was freedom from that uphill battle known as adulthood. The one that included taking care of me and not even minding. Childhood was pure pink and roses (except for school), and I loved it. Indeed, I cherished it.

I was eleven and three quarters years old, the day I was forced to remove my white undershirt for the last time, and put on that first bra.

When I left the department store in downtown Oakland, CA, my chest now encased in a contraption that constricted my lungs so tightly I could barely breathe, I knew it was over. I wasn't a kid anymore. I was suddenly…I didn't know exactly. But what I *did* know, with blinding certainty, I was heading toward something serious, stifling and dangerous.

I had no desire to grow up. I wasn't looking to leave home. I wasn't looking to try grown up things.

I wasn't into dabbing on my mother's perfume, or her lipstick. Even though I was entranced when she wore perfume.

And she wore lipstick so expertly she didn't need a mirror to apply it.

I wasn't secretly dancing around in her high heels, craning to see myself in the mirror.

When I leafed through her McCall's magazine, it was to get to the Betsy McCall paper doll page.

So I most certainly wasn't holding my breath and counting the days until breasts sprouted and joyfully leapt into a bra. I wasn't that girl.

Because, in spite of being a new kid at a different school every three years, I had it good and I knew it. I liked my life at home with Mom in charge, baby sisters, great snacks and lots of books. In spite of the periodic uprooting, life was easy, safe and interesting.

Even so, my breasts bloomed right on schedule. I was horrified, so I ignored their polite little hellos from there on *my* chest. I continued to wear my undershirts. My mother noticed, but was busy with my younger brother and sisters and a looming move from Oakland, CA to Brussels, Belgium, which involved among other things, dragging all five of us kids over to San Francisco where we spent an entire day procuring our passports. I can see my undershirt beneath my blouse in my passport picture.

But life marches on like a squalling infant who's started to sprout teeth. She cries because subliminally she knows this little happening spells the end to breast feeding.

The fact is, I was shamed into getting my first bra. Unfortunately, I'm the sort who always has to be shamed or dragged into the next phase of life, whatever that may be.

I'm not proud of this, okay?

It was a sunny morning in school at the end of sixth grade. Sr. Daniel Marie had just handed out the assignment. I was minding my own business, when suddenly I noticed, under the almost transparent school uniform blouse of the girl sitting in front of me, a tiny line of bra right across the center of her back. She was Pamela Quinn, the smallest kid in existence. If you weren't staring at the ground, you'd trip over her. She was wearing a bra? Where'd she get it? In the doll department? I began to think I didn't know Pamela Quinn at all. She totally had to be faking it.

But then I took a slow look around the classroom, and to my growing horror, there under every white blouse of every single girl in the room, I saw the same tell-tale white line across their back.

The world dropped out from underneath me.

The classroom was suddenly filled with bras. Did this mean they were *ahead* of me in all kinds of scary, sociologically accurate ways? Were they onto something? Like that year I was way ahead of everyone when I got the first Betsy McCall doll in my neighborhood? Were they…cooler than me?

No!

I surreptitiously touched my wonderful easy-going undershirt. But instead of comfort, a silent bleat of alarm rose up. When had this happened? *When had I been left behind?*

This was yet another year in which I was a new kid. This meant I had a lot of superficial friends. I got invited to parties, and all, particularly when the word got out that the new kid was already moving away (easy come, easy go), and not only was I moving away, I was moving away to that most glamorous place, Europe. I had become a minor celebrity before I had a chance to make a soul mate friend. We all know how hard it is for celebrities to make friends, right?

So all around me my "friends", whom I now realized I

knew nothing about, had gone out with their Moms and gotten their first bras. And never told me. Of course this was California, where it is notoriously difficult to make soul mate friends. There seems to be a waiting period of ten years for that to occur, so maybe they hadn't even told each other.

But nonetheless, a kind of mass consciousness had occurred. And I hadn't been in on it.

I sat there, rooted to the spot, as I gaped at all those bras underneath all those white blouses.

I clutched my desk, as Sr. Daniel Marie droned on about something meaningless. I was the last to know. It was bad to be the last to know. I was an experienced new kid, in which being the last to know is in the job description. But also in the job description is being alert to whatever the lastest fads are in the new school. Fastest way to make a friend is to be the *first* to know. Even my eight year-old brother knew that, in this, his third new school

I could have gotten a bra months before. I *should* have gotten a bra six months before. I *had* sprouted. Nothing gigantic. But certainly enough to qualify. My mother had even cautiously broached the subject. But I had barked her down, and she, already having enough children to keep happy, backed off.

I'd barked because I didn't want to qualify for a bra. My first bra. Bells did not go off at the thought. I did not want something clamped around my chest.

I didn't want to grow up—

There, I said it.

To absolutely no avail.

I sat there in my seat in that school in Oakland, CA, slowly shriveling up as my future loomed.

What was it going to be next? Getting my period? I knew

about those. I knew about a lot of things about a woman's body. Including how babies came out. One day I asked my mother when she was eight months pregnant with one of my younger sisters. She got down on the floor and demonstrated from where the human emerges. I was appalled. But I also loved my mother so much at that moment because I knew she would always tell me the truth about these things, not fairy tales. Then she lumbered back up to her feet, laughing. "Don't worry," she said. "It's always okay, and then you have a new baby." My brave mother!

But back to the threat at hand…wasn't life bad enough, that just as I was getting settled in Oakland, CA, my father was moving us all the way over to Brussels, Belgium? Even Mom was upset. But now this?

Obviously Mother Nature didn't care.

And so here I was.

"Mom, I need to get a bra." I practically choked on the words. I think Mom was cooking dinner. I think she had a fretting, teething one year old latched onto her right hip.

"Okay," she said. "Are you sure, though? I asked you before and you got mad."

Who me? Mad?

"Every girl in my whole class has a bra already," I muttered. "And a couple of them don't even need one." I spit that last out. I didn't actually understand it, but that was the moment I realized there were girls obviously cooler than me, and furthermore, there were always going to be girls obviously cooler than me.

Eleven is a brutal age.

So there I was in a department store with Mom, who was

busily summoning a saleswoman to come measure me for that new bra. We'd come with no baby sisters. I have no idea where she left them or what it had taken for her to get out of the house with only one child, her sullen eleven year old. However, she'd done it, but now she was in no mood to put up with any signs of temper from me. I was to grin and bear it, what ever it might take.

"Oh my yes," said the beaming saleswoman at me. She was old, at least forty, but very self-assured. I guess bra saleswomen have to be. "Do you have anything on under your blouse?"

I cleared my throat. "An undershirt," I whispered. And I was as sure as I was eleven years old that I was not going to take off that undershirt.

"Good," she said. "Let's go into a dressing room now. Where I would like you to take off your blouse so I can measure you." This was a statement.

I hated her. I was a private person, couldn't she see? I was a real person, for that matter. One who should not be made to publicly humiliate herself in this stupid department store. I was not going to take my blouse off for some bully of a saleswoman who wanted to embarrass me.

My mother cleared her throat. There was a dangerous note to it. We arrived at a dressing room. The saleswoman held open the curtain. I stood there. Mom cleared her throat again. My mother was a Southerner. They speak foreign languages fluently with one clearing of their throats. I stepped into the dressing room and the sales woman stepped in with me. Was she kidding? She actually thought she could stand there while I as good as got naked? "Do you mind waiting outside until I have my blouse off?" I know my voice was strangled. She must have heard it, so with the tiniest of shrugs, maybe the tiniest of knowing smiles, out she stepped. Where my mother, wisely, was waiting.

I looked at my face for a long time. It looked the same. The freckles were still there. The hair was still brown, the eyes blue, the mouth set sternly. This was the last time I would see it as the face of a carefree kid. The last time as the girl who could get dressed in the morning and run out the door without having to put on a bra. The girl who could run free and loose in the forest of life and play, without some strangle hold around her chest.

I unbuttoned my school uniform blouse, took it off and hung it on the hanger. I sputtered for the saleswoman and her tape measurer to come back in and violate me. With a brisk rustle she did. She wrapped that tape measurer around my chest as I held my breath and looked away. Her face was much too big, much too close to mine. "32 AA," she said loudly to my mother through the curtain.

And thus, quickly and efficiently, did my childhood end.

When I left that dressing room that day, wearing my first bra, a scarlet letter was emblazoned on my forehead, and I was an innocent child no more. I was wearing a bra, a woman's bra, and therefore throwing my newborn chest out into the ring of who had the biggest, the best, the roundest, the pinkest, the sexiest, the smallest, the end all be all, in the breast contest of life. Mom took me for an ice cream cone, and talked about school, her own mother, what Belgium might be like—anything but the iron chain now hanging like the biggest bully in the world, around my no longer kid like chest.

They're right here right now, with me, my loyal breasts.

They grew to their perfect size. They've been kissed, fondled, and in general, lavished over by the select few. They have breast fed two demanding babies, who were both upset when breast feeding came to an end. They've been tanned to perfection, they've been mammogrammed as infrequently as I can get away with, they've gained weight and lost weight, all the while showing up everyday of my life to hang out with me. They are as old as I am, and go everywhere with me.

Right now they are clad in a gorgeous black bra.

Wondering what all the fuss was about, way back then.

SPANX

Spanx?

What the heck was Spanx? The word was on everyone's lips. Was it pornographic? It certainly sounded pornographic.

I'm right, right? About the pornographic part?

Spanx turned out to be the secret behind all those women wearing their skin tight dresses with not even a hint of flab, tummy or panty line showing. I had never understood how that was even possible. I went around fretting about it. I did. And then one day I heard about—

Spanx.

Okay, so, I'm not a neophyte when it comes to women's artifice for achieving physical perfection and/or just getting through the day. I never fell behind again in this department after the first bra debacle.

I am completely savvy when it comes to what somebody has injected into their face. Or if that perfect body is from Pilates or weightlifting or running marathons. Or if those eyes scream still smoking too much pot or guzzling the vodka. Or the pills. You know with pills—that confused, dry mouth conversation and all?

But obviously somehow, some way, I'd slipped. Here I was. Late again, to the lingerie party.

It really all started with white cotton underpants. Puritan chic is what I call white cotton underpants.

Lingerie in my life was defined early on by my mother. Maybe because she had six children and white cotton underpants simply made life easier, but I did not have stars on my underpants, or teddy bears or balloons or the days of the week painted on them. My underpants were not cute. They weren't what all the other girls had. I didn't even have plain pink, yellow or blue. I had white cotton underpants. I also had white curtains in my bedroom windows, white cotton sheets, and a white quilted bedspread on my bed. So the theme was deeply embedded. I wore plain white cotton underpants, day in and day out, all through my childhood. Which occurred in the great New England state of Massachusetts.

I didn't resent it exactly. In the first place I didn't know the word 'resent' existed. Nor did I go around questioning what my mother's rules or her way of doing things. For instance, Christmas morning. We opened our gifts *after* Mass, *after* breakfast. We opened them one at a time, oohing and ahhing over each gift as it emerged. So we were the last ones on the block opening our gifts, while everyone else was already outside yelling about what they'd gotten. I felt sorry for them. Because in our living room the best part of Christmas day was still going on. There were six kids. So eventually this tradition took a long time. It reached its peak when the ritual began to include new spouses. One year we were still opening gifts at 1:00pm and had to break for lunch. Luxurious. Decadent.

However eventually I realized I might be missing out. I realized I was the only girl I knew who didn't have Hallmark cute underpants. I wasn't sure I liked this. So I girded my loins and asked my mother why it was she only got me white underwear. This was at a time when I didn't ask my parents for anything lightly lest it take away the ability to ask, beg or plead for a serious need, like a must-have toy. I didn't want to hear "Okay, you can have balloons on your underpants, but forget about that new Ginny doll and three fantabulous outfits for her."

I was watching my mother put my carefully folded underpants in my chest of drawers when I asked her about this issue of embellished underwear. She paused. It seemed this was a brand new concept to her. The concept of balloons on my underpants, polka dots, stars, kittens. Or the concept that I may actually want something like that. I wasn't sure. "You want underpants with things printed on them?" she asked, her lovely face swinging to have a closer look at me, her Southern lilt still very much a part of her, in spite of the snow outside, the lobster stands around the corner, the mittens. Maybe I was sick? Was I upset?

My nine year old face was purposefully bland. "I just want to know why you only get me white ones," I said carefully, a new Ginny doll on my mind.

There was a pause. Then she closed the drawer. "Well, I think those colorful ones look cheap," she said. "The white cotton underpant is simple and classic and always looks good," she said. She straightened up, not quite looking at me. "But if you want balloons on your underpants, I'll get you some."

Of course I didn't want balloons on my underwear. Definitely I did not want kittens on my underwear. Most definitely I didn't want anything that looked cheap to my mother anywhere near my body. And most definitely I wanted that new Ginny doll.

I grew up and got married when I was nineteen.

Ridiculous. I know that now. But our parents, worried we'd elope if they said 'no', reluctantly went through the process of getting two nineteen year olds married.

My mother pulled me aside one day. "I have a present for you." We sat down on her bed, and she handed me a gorgeous box from Joseph's. Joseph's was the crème de la crème of department stores in downtown Pasadena, California. My mind sparkled with what might be inside. I opened the gift up slowly, savoring whatever was to come. Oh such lovely tissue paper. Such a beautiful silk bow. I opened it up, and lifted the pale aqua tissue paper and beheld my gift. I sucked my breath in, and looked up at my mother.

Because inside were two exquisite pairs of underpants. Only these could not be called underpants. They were not white cotton. They were lingerie in all the sensual opulence the word implies. Lingerie for a woman. A woman getting married. Two enchanting pairs. For a moment I just stared at them. Then I lifted them out carefully.

One was like a Monet painting of his water lilies, all sky blues and watery greens. Flowers. Delicate lacing. Tiny bows. The other was rose and pink and pearly grays. Slightly larger bow and wider lace trim. Both pairs were the most gorgeous things I'd ever seen in my life. Redolent of Paris, Chanel #5, chandeliers, filagree, gossamer.

I swooned. "Mom, thank you! Thank you!" She smiled her enigmatic smile. I felt like she was finally acknowledging me as a woman, even though she knew I was rushing things. She would be there to catch me when I fell, but in the meantime, she was giving me my first truly grown up gift from her.

"I hope you like them," she said, her soft drawl crooning the words, her lovely smile deepening even more.

They were so beautiful I didn't wear either pair for quite awhile. My new husband finally dared me to.

Those two pairs of perfect panties lasted a very long time. They outlasted any number of pairs of panties that had all sorts of flowers and stars and polka dots and pop art on them.

The beauties were even machine washable—my mother would have been too practical to get me anything that wasn't.

I hand washed them anyway.

Which brings me to pantyhose, on my journey towards Spanx.

Or rather, the days before the existence of panty hose.

Do you remember those days? Like yesterday? Ah well…

My personal need for pantyhose arose in the sixties when mini skirts were invented. It was Twiggy's fault. When I started wearing miniskirts it was winter…in Pasadena, California, so it could have been worse, but you couldn't tell me that.

Remember garter belts? They made wearing miniskirts uncomfortable and dangerous because it was impossible to wear garters and hose underneath them without the garters showing. Life is tough when you're sixteen, getting ready for the Dave Clark Five concert or the Beatle concert or the Rolling Stone concert, with the perfect mini-skirt to wear, but having to switch to bellbottoms at the last minute because the stupid garters showed.

So, sixteen years old, and pre-panty-hose, was tough and anxiety-driven. Especially when my mother came home from London with a real Carnaby Street mini-dress just for me. It was sugar. It had dimples, it was so cute. It was a pink and white checked gingham with belled sleeves. It was short. Oh so blissfully short. It was perfect. I was thrilled. Mom beamed.

This was also the time of girdles. Girdles, which also had garter like clips for holding up stockings. But girdles, as opposed to garters, were shorter, and so could be hidden by the mini-skirt. I had to borrow my mother's girdle because she absolutely refused to buy me one. "You don't need a girdle."

"Yes I do, for stockings when I wear my dresses."

"You'll hate it."

"I need it for your Carnaby Street dress, Mom." She lent me her girdle.

But the girdle was indeed awful. I did hate it. I suffocated in it. I was a trussed up goose ready for baking. I couldn't breathe. I knew the world could see I was encased, gasping for air, in my mother's girdle. This was an impossible situation. If only summer would come. Then the need for stockings would become a moot point.

But winter persisted, the year I got my real live London Carnaby Street mini-dress. So I brooded. I moped. I considered giving up until summer. And then one day I had a flash. I tried out flesh colored tights (which also proved hard to find), hoping they would pass for stockings. My boyfriend thought they looked stupid. They did. I wore the dress once. I prayed some more for summer—

And then one day, a miracle blew in to the world of female sanity. Out of nowhere, pantyhose arrived. They blew into our daily life like eagles, like jet planes, like true love. A brand new world was ushered in! Undergarment woes were solved, and women could now conquer the world.

I could conquer the world...

Until last year when I bought a skin-tight dress to wear to a wedding.

I saw a woman one day at the car wash on Pacific Coast Highway across from the Balboa Yacht Club, who, for no good reason I could see, had chosen to wear her own skin tight dress to get her car dolled up. This dress clung to her body with nary an imperfection. I'm known for accosting a stranger if for some reason, good or bad, they've caught my attention. I said, "Excuse me, where are your panty lines?" My envy was evident. My tone cool and yes, hostile. Perfection wasn't required or even expected at the car wash. I could only imagine what this woman looked like when she really wanted to impress.

She turned to me, not a skin-tight feather ruffled, and replied in a foreign language. "Spanx," she said.

I looked at her. "Spanks?" I asked. "Like spank with a paddle?"

"S. P. A. N. X." said the woman, not a glimmer of a smile. The lack of smile clued me in right then and there that, in spite of the giant X in the picture, I had just been let in on the biggest secret I never knew existed. The Secret of Spanx. The Cult of Spanx. The Scientology of Spanx. Apparently this moronically named item of women's undergarments, this phenomena that took every imperfection out of the skin-tight dress, was waiting for me at my local department store, and had been for a long time. I smiled. Solutions, ergo Nirvana, right there at my fingertips.

Which lead me to breakfast at Café Zinc's, in Laguna Beach, California, where I called upon my friends to corroborate this miracle called Spanx.

"You've never heard of Spanx?" They were open-mouthed.

"Never," I said, sipping my latte with aplomb. I did know

how to maneuver the coffee order. "So," I said, knowing my friends very well, "I need your help." The table went quiet. They leaned in. "I need you to tell me what to do to get some."

No one was smiling anymore. This was serious business. This was…important.

"Absolutely be sure to go to Bloomingdales and ask for, no wait…demand Salli. She knows how to fit a woman for Spanx."

"Absolutely get one a size too small. It has to be really hard to pull on. Really hard, okay?"

"Absolutely be sure to get one that gets your whole torso or you'll regret it."

"Absolutely be sure to get one that gets your thighs, or you'll regret it."

"Absolutely be sure to actually try it on. Don't buy it off the rack."

"Hey, get more than one."

"Absolutely be sure to go to Neiman Marcus and ask for…no, demand Danni. She knows how to fit a woman for Spanx."

I went to Macy's because I didn't want to run into anybody I knew. I needed to focus.

I don't know about your Macy's. But my Macy's has been gradually going downhill. Whereas long ago it used to be somebody, now it isn't. Lingerie has been moved down to the lower level. In other places this floor is called the basement, but since there aren't basements in California, what this means is it merely feels like a basement because the ceilings are lower, and opens onto the lower parking lot.

I strode into the underwear department in the basement of Macy's. It glared under overhead fluorescent light. I could easily see the shadows under my eyes as I passed by the strategic mirror here and there. I stopped looking. I passed tables mounded with manhandled underpants. I did not stop to see if white cotton underwear was lurking. I brushed passed displays of bras in every shape and color, but with none my size. Which was a good thing. I didn't need another bra I'd bought without trying on. Okay…I haven't done that in years. Ever since I realized my cup size was changing. Not only my cup size, but the spread of my back, my underarm pits, and where my waist was now, for some mysterious reason (okay, scoliosis) was newly located. I could go on, but—

I was here to buy a Spanx. Spanx, which ends in an 'x', and how cute was that-

When suddenly, there they were!

The real thing.

The real deal.

Spanks with an 'x'. I gazed, awe preparing to leap into my eyes, to envelop my very being—

But…but…they looked like my mother's girdle. My determination skidded to a halt, and my spirit downshifted.

I knew they were Spanx, not girdles, because there was a sign hanging over them saying so. They were hanging up on the wall, not crammed and folded on kiosks for the whole world to manhandle. I felt a small return of spirit. I'd been expecting them to be hidden away in a corner so that you wouldn't be seen buying one. Because I still had it in my head that Spanx was a huge secret. I mean why else was this miracle news to me. I believe in Botox. I'm not a nun.

Unfortunately though, the Spanx themselves, didn't blow me away.

But what had I expected? Had I honestly thought a delicate shiver of lace would be able to accomplish what these suits of armor were designed to do?

Looking closer I saw that they were bigger than girdles, in fact. They were more convoluted, higher tech, more complex than the mere girdle. They were the skyscraper of underpinnings. I felt my chest tighten. I felt my breath tighten. I felt gasping and choking coming on. Because these Spanx things were odes to everything bad about women's perceptions of their bodies. They were odes to a perfection that was not normal to obtain. There they hung. Personifications of a backward slide for all Women's Lib had tried to change—

My ears started to hurt. I wanted to run—

But then, I pulled myself together.

I told myself that I didn't care that men never stuffed their own paunches into such life-sucking contraptions

Visions of my oh so sexy dress sliding down my newly flattened hips and stomach burst into my mind's eye like a murmuration of starlings, only more beautiful. *Yes! Do it,* I yelled deep within. I wanted this dress to fit more than I wanted the right to vote. *Face it!* Nothing but nothing was more important than how I looked at this wedding!

So I took a deep breath, stood in front of this wall of iron maidens, and tried to get my bearings. I didn't want to be bothered by a salesperson. I could figure it out. I needed to slide down this rabbit hole alone. The sizing couldn't be too obscure, could it? It would just take me a minute to get oriented...

"Can I help you?"

A wail went through my heart. Noooo! Sales person. I was exposed. I'd been seen-

But I knew what I wanted, right?

I closed my eyes, took a breath, then turned to face the sales person. She looked like Edith Bunker, except tall. Her face was almost stern, as if to say 'I know who you are. You are one of those uptight women who believes she knows what she's doing when it comes to buying foundation garments, so doesn't need the help of someone who actually does know what she's doing.' She repeated the question. "Can I help you?"

She knew the right answer. She knew that I knew the right answer. I glanced back at the wall of girdle-like Spanx. I yielded.

"Yes," I muttered. "I need a Spanx."

She could have said 'No kidding, since here you stand staring at a wall of Spanx,', but instead she eyed me up and down. "You look like you're between a six and an eight, she said."

"I have a size six dress I must get into for a wedding," I blurted.

She eyed me up and down again. "That's possible," she said at last, and I could have kissed her. She asked me to describe the dress. "It would have been better if you'd brought the dress with you, of course," she said. Then she turned to the wall and stared at it, thoughtfully clucking ever so softly, before diving in and pulling out four likely suspects.

She led the way to the dressing rooms. She brushed open the curtains to an empty one, handed me the Spanx, and told me to call if I needed anything. "They should fit you really tightly. They should feel too small." I nodded earnestly. She was going to leave me to it. She wasn't going to hover. I could have kissed her again.

She left. And I was alone in the dressing room.

I turned to the four nylon and spandex suits of armor hanging there. They gazed back at me balefully. They were beige, or maybe ecru. They were not pretty. They were not sexy. They were not for the romantic evening out. They were tough, street smart and unflappable—

Just like me, right?

I removed my clothes and one by one, while gradually working up a sweat, I painfully dragged on each breath sucker, muscle cramping, svelte inducing contraption. Then, equally as exhaustingly, I dragged each one off. What I would do when actually out in public wearing the thing, needing to go to the bathroom, I chose to ignore. Whether I should wear my pantyhose over or under the Spanx was a question I would also wrestle with later. I didn't even think of worrying if my dress would cover the Spanx.

What mattered now was would Spanx do the job?

This is murder, I thought. Murder to my psyche, murder in the first. This is very very bad, I thought. The Spanx(es?) hung there, looking the worse for wear. But I had to do it. I had to buy a Spanx. Vanity was to be given its due too.

Like the time I told my daughter that Botox would help her be in a better mood when she looked in the mirror because that frown crater between her eyebrows would be all gone…

I picked one. Then I got dressed, picked up my purse, and marched confidently out to the counter to purchase it. "Ahh, this is a good one," said the tall saleswoman. "You'll never regret it."

Two weeks later, with the help of my brand new Spanx, and three times a week Zumba classes for good measure, I shimmied into my dress and slithered sveltely off to the wedding.

It was sooooooo worth it. So very very worth it!

Spanx.

With an *X*.

⌒⌒⌒

New Babies

Babies are cherry pink and milk chocolate and tan as summer sunshine, or white and blue or black as midnight, sweetly scented with baby powder, smiling heaps of adoration and cooing in your direction, almost all the time…if memory serves me correctly. Human babies' adorableness is almost equal to that of the exquisite adorableness of kittens meowing as they skitter from you in a hopeless display of furry self-reliance, dropping like confused lemmings off the edge of your willing lap, landing with a whisper. Nothing but nothing is cuter than kittens…sorry, babies.

But I digress.

I always wanted my own babies. I loved them. They were cuter than cute, oh so sweet, and I got to play with them as much as I wanted. There were six siblings in my family. I had three much younger sisters, so there was always one of those absolutely pink and pretty babies tottering around. The baby had curly hair. The baby gurgled, cooed and laughed. The baby had wonder in her eyes.

And my mother swooped her up when the going got rough.

I had to learn the hard way I had no grasp at all of what my mother's daily life had entailed herding six children.

My husband and I were reluctantly allowed to get married at the appalling ages of nineteen and twenty. We were idiots. So it is amazing we were in no hurry to have children any time soon. Or I should say I suddenly was in no hurry.

This surprised me. But the married thing had turned out to be work enough. I was no longer the only person in my life. The desire for my own baby flew quietly away. Very very far away.

It wasn't until we'd been married seven years that we got around to "deciding" to have a baby. So it came to be that during a wildly romantic week-end in New Orleans we gorged on oysters, drank gin till we knew how to make it, and made love till we'd beaten all previous records. Somewhere in there we also threw away our birth control. Eh voila, I thought. Baby time!

No.

It took two years, two long, confusing years to get pregnant. I was beside myself. My husband pretended to wring his hands. I read many many many pregnancy books.

And then, one weekend I went with him on a business trip to Neptune, New Jersey, where voila! we got pregnant as if it was the easiest thing in the world to do. It was a Saturday morning, in the nondescript motel where we were staying.

Motels were the magic wand, apparently, because less than two years later we got pregnant with the second baby, on another Saturday morning, in another nondescript motel, on another business trip, this time in Baltimore, MD. Again we got pregnant as if it was the easiest thing in the world to do.

My son, my firstborn, arrived, and they put him in my arms. I lost my breath from the wonder of it. Feeling my newborn's breath on my neck made me dizzy. New breath.

Brand new breath coming forth from this tiny, new human being my husband and I had just created. This was new life, right here, right now. Living breathing.

I couldn't breathe myself. A mere week before, he had still been in utero, still not out amongst us. A year ago he hadn't even been on here on earth.

But now, here was a new human being, and my husband and I had done this. It seemed sacrilegious, this power.

What if we slipped up with this responsibility?

Not quite two years later, I felt my newborn daughter's breath on my neck. Again I felt raw unbridled awe at the arrival of this new human being. A new human being here on earth, because of me. Because of my husband and I having sex. Again the miracle of life stopped me. And again I wondered if I was up for the job. If I was up for the molding and fashioning this beautiful, complete innocent into a functioning human being. Making sure I was adding a good person and a moral person to this world's population.

This time, though, I was not innocent myself of all that would go into this marathon of raising a child. I was not a newborn mother myself. I had a twenty-month baby boy at home, waiting for me, so very not ready to be sent off on his own while I got a handle on the new baby.

Suddenly, there, moments after giving birth, I saw twenty years at least stretching out in front of me, filled, every step of the way with new hurdles, new confusions, new joys, but oh so many tears coming from, what had been just one baby, to now, a simple snap of the fingers, two babies. All because my husband and I had sex on those Saturday mornings, on business trips, in nondescript motels.

I saw white. I heard buzzing. I started to choke. Panic rose. I looked wildly up at my husband and through the thundering in my head, minutes after our daughter had taken her first breath, I gasped "No sex until you've had a vasectomy." I tried to breathe. My husband hovered over me. He was as wild eyed as I was. He nodded. He nodded vigorously, clutching my hand, sweat beginning to drop off his formerly calm face—

Nurses moved in to allay the panic.

And so it was, two weeks later, on a snowy Monday morning, in Baltimore, MD, I put our infant daughter and twenty month old son into their baby seats in the car, eased my still pregnancy hungry body into the car, and drove my husband to the hospital where the job would be done.

I dropped him off. A friend would pick him up that afternoon. And I shakily drove through the newly fallen snow, barely making it up the hill to our house, got the babies out of the car one at a time, and went in.

Therein ensued the classic infant/toddler morning of breastfeeding, bottle feeding, lunch for the toddler, more breastfeeding for the infant, the holding thereof of each child for what seemed like hours at a time, the rocking, the changing of diapers, the talking to the son, the cooing to the daughter, and then all over again. I didn't brush my hair. I barely manage a cup of decaffeinated coffee. I think I watched very early Oprah. I desperately tried to get the toddler enthralled with the Muppets. He wasn't. He was too young. He sucked his thumb instead, and wanted me to read to him. I looked around the kitchen, and knew not despair. I was too tired for anything so strong as despair. I looked around dazed. Completely and totally dazed.

Then right on cue, the infant woke up, and began her tiny mewls and squeals, which alerted my toddler who'd been watching me like a hawk ever since the alien presence had entered his formerly peaceful home. I, breathing for calm, put my infant to my breast, hoping I was emanating calm Mother Earth vibes, so she could grow up to be strong and sure. My toddler popped his thumb out of his mouth and with a steely look in his dethroned-baby eyes, started to crawl onto my lap. The infant sputtered at my breast and started to wail. Thumb popped out of his mouth and the toddler started to wail too.

What had happened? When did this happen? I had always wanted children. Beautiful, fully bathed and clothed and fed and brought to the doctor's appointments and laughing all the time, happy babies. Laughing, giggling, chirping babies, wearing absolutely adorable clothes—

Obviously I had wanted them in the abstract.

The first time I introduced solid food to my five-month old son, he and I, and the husband too, had individual nervous breakdowns. There seemed no way to get it right. And no one had warned me.

Oh, my friends had been very sure it was time he started on solids. That it was time for solids in addition to the breast feeding to continue his steady and sturdy growth into adulthood. But they didn't warn me that baby would not understand in the slightest what I was trying to do to him when I tentatively aimed that first spoonful of baby cereal into his adorable little mouth. I had no idea he would wave his little fists, scrunch up his face, and gag on the mush as I tried to spoon it into his mouth. That he would spit and choke and try to cry, dribbling baby cereal out of his mouth like he'd just had a baby version of a stroke. I was fragile, too. I would have broken down in tears except hubby was trying to take cute pictures.

I brought the next spoonful up to his mouth. My husband dutifully snapped away. In the pictures you can't see that my armpits are sweating. My upper lip was sweating. Probably my baby was sweating.

It was a shock to find out baby didn't automatically know how to eat—

Although I wonder why now, because the beginning of nursing him had been a nightmare.

The books just show pretty pictures of mother and child nursing. A lot of soft lace and plush blankets, just a touch of breast, the back of the seemingly enthralled infant's head. But it turns out this beatific scene happens weeks after the start. After weeks of practice, sweat, blood and tears.

The first moments after birth, nursing my son had been picture book perfect. But on the third day my milk flooded in, and my breasts went from normal, 34B breasts happily at one with this breast-feeding scheme, to giant, rocklike, 16FFF, football breasts. And it was from these now giant human edifices bulging from my chest, my tiny infant was supposed to nurse.

Well he couldn't. My infant son could not hang on to the nipple. Because my nipples were now as large as his head. The breasts themselves were larger than his head. He'd try to suck from my shocked and rigid nipples. Nothing would happen because he couldn't get a good enough grasp to suck hard enough. I tried to encourage my three day old son to suck like Superman, but he apparently didn't understand English. Or hadn't been born with an awareness of Superman.

Suddenly the milk would let down in a powerful geyser and knock his three-day-old lips right off the nipple and out of the ballpark. The milk would then squirt into his nose and eyes. He would choke, gasp, then wail in shock.

Nurses, beautiful nurses, rushed to our aid. Apparently I wasn't the first with this problem. I wasn't? How come nobody talked about this issue? This very pertinent issue of the difficulty of breast feeding the newborn because the breasts are so engorged with new milk they have become boulders of frustration on your own chest. They were so big they probably scared my newborn. They scared me. They scared my husband. I was too overwrought to even contemplate what this was actually doing to the breasts themselves.

But it was too late anyway. I had this baby. I was determined to breastfeed him.

And what had been softly imagined as a pure and beautiful thing had become this carnival sideshow.

For the first three weeks, I held him under my arm like a football, so the angle of the ginormous nipples would be easier for his tiny rosebud of a mouth to get a grip on. My husband did not take any pictures of this.

But it did all settle down nicely, so that breastfeeding did end up being the wonderful experience I had envisioned. And indeed, it went well, from the start, with baby number two.

So that too, I tried to assured myself, this feeding of solid food to my baby would ultimately soon be the norm and it wouldn't faze me.

But after I fed him, and after I had cleaned him and me up, and after my husband had taken him for a walk, both of us worried he'd hadn't had enough to eat, a thick wave of despair rolled over me. "I have another eighteen more years of force feeding my child, three times a day," I said out loud to the refrigerator, in front of which I was standing, dazed and woozy. "I'm not going to make it, I whispered." I clutched at the open door of my formally comforting refrigerator.

Because even at that moment, when I only had to choose between baby cereal and breast milk for my baby's meal, and I only had one baby for which I was going to have to do this, I realized like a sledgehammer swinging right at me, that the making of all those soon to be more complicated meals was going to be a long hard slog.

Which is also never mentioned in baby books.

I don't know how women survive. And I really don't know why women lie about the truth of early babyhood to their sisters. By sisters, I mean all fellow women, particularly those of the same age group.

Every time a woman, with three toddlers screaming around her feet, rings two feet deep under her eyes, accumulated baby fat clinging to her entire body, even her chin, if she'd had the energy to notice, looks me right in the eye and says, "I've never been happier", I stare back and think 'liar.'

I wonder why she doesn't have the nerve to admit she's miserable, because then she could reach out for that hug she so desperately needs, the hug where someone else is doing the soothing patting. This woman loves her toddlers, of that I have no doubt. As did I mine. But having this motherhood dream and finding out it's not one bit like the fairytales, well it isn't a sin to scream to high heaven the job is harder than you ever thought. That it is the hardest thing you've ever done. And that eighty-five percent of the time it's no fun.

My sense of humor deserted me. Anxiety blossomed, thoroughly watered everyday by the never-ending details and questions and hurdles and changes that occurred with this new motherhood job. I agonized over every single detail that came with the job. The biggest one being a constant fear that I was somehow, unwittingly, going to harm my baby, thereby ruining his life forever.

It was exhausting.

I was walking my two babies one cold day in Chicago. Neither of them ever liked to be taken on walks in their carriage. Nor were they the type of baby who fell sweetly asleep in their car seats. This day they were both in the carriage, a handsome spectacle my mother had hauled out of the attic. I hadn't yet discovered those handy dandy umbrella strollers. My infant daughter was squalling. My twenty month old son was huddled next to her, thumb in his mouth, looking at me, his eyes so filled with reproach, I would have laughed if I had remembered how.

We passed a woman who was the age I am now. An elegant woman, looking calm and unflustered, her winter coat tied so perfectly around her waist, her knitted cap and gloves claiming a dignity only an older woman can lend to a knitted cap and gloves. She smiled at bedraggled me and stopped to look in at my picture perfect scene of wailing babydom. She smiled at the two of them. They paid her no attention. My daughter continued to wail. My son continued to haul ass on his thumb, his huge blue eyes never leaving my face. She straightened up and looked at me. She had such calm, intelligent, and kind eyes, I could have wept right there. She took my hand in hers. "These can be ghastly days. But it will get better," she said. "Maybe not soon, but it *will* get better. I was where you are now, and it got better." She gave my hand a steadying squeeze. Her eyes smiled at me. And then she was gone.

A calm, warm peace reached in and soothed my exhausted heart.

That moment of complete empathy carried me through until the moment when raising my babies did get better. That moment of understanding from an experienced mother once removed, was perfume for my psyche. I've never forgotten that moment or that woman who, unsolicited, said the very thing I desperately needed to hear.

So now, when I see a young mother with two or three babies under the age of three, and she has that stunned look of quiet desperation in her eyes, after smiling at her wet and snotty offspring, I say to her, "It will get better. Maybe not soon, but it *will* get better." And never once has one reared back and demanded to know just what the hell I was talking about? Instead, every time, a small look of exhausted gratitude with just a glimmer of hope has made its way into her eyes.

Because while it is true our babies are cherry pink, chocolate velvet, and smell so sweetly of roses and apple blossoms, they are tiny, completely helpless beings, and the raising of these tiny creatures is the most formidable enterprise an adult human being will ever undertake.

Everest

One summer I went away to camp in Geneva, Switzerland. I was thirteen. I desperately wanted to go to this camp—
   And ended up hating every minute I was there.
   They threw me in with the older girls. These fourteen and fifteen year old girls thought I was three years old, and so I didn't stand a chance. At home I was the oldest daughter in a family of six. I ran the place. Not at this high-strung prison. I was picked on or ignored, and remained basically friendless the whole time. If ever I wished I was a year younger and could have been with the twelve year olds, it was that summer.
   But the night before we were to go home there was a dance. Boys and girls got to mingle. The older girls all dressed fast and ran on ahead of me. I thought about staying in the room. But no. I knew boys at dances. I never had problems on my own turf. The boys didn't know I was only thirteen. I was tall for my age. And I was sure the girls wouldn't have me on their minds.
   So heck yeah I went! And I was a hit! The boys saw something the nasty older girls missed. I danced the whole night. In particular there was this one boy named Charles...
   But that was the last night. Before that had been three weeks of well...camp misery.

The camp wasn't for sissies. It was up in the Alps, above Lake Geneva. The itinerary included hiking mountains, which also included climbing so high in the Alps one time we hit tundra. It looked like a moonscape, and was momentarily flat, so for a brief moment we hiked easily, and I think even the nasty girls were spellbound by the environment.

I took horseback riding lessons down at the edge of Lake Geneva, and these lessons were taught by a veritable Hun. Barking discipline was his style. One time I fell off my horse. Before I knew what hit me, before I could even consider a whimper, he was by my head roaring "Get up! Get back on zee haas. Immediately!" I threw myself up at the horse, spitting sawdust out of my mouth, praying I'd make it all the way up.

And then there was Everest. This was the giant high dive at Lake Geneva where we went swimming everyday after horseback riding with Herr Hun.

It was an Olympic height diving platform for those of us wishing to risk our lives jumping off the top. I was part of the group who wished to risk my life jumping off the top, even though I couldn't breathe once I got all the way up.

Day after day, I'd climb all the way up to the top because, after going off the two sissy lower levels, I knew, I just knew that to give my life meaning and hope, I'd have to jump off the top of the diving platform.

But day after day I tiptoed shakily over to the edge, looked down at the hard water miles below, and slunk shakily back.

Then the last day of camp arrived. This should have been cause for celebration. But I alone, of those up there giving it a go, I alone had not taken the plunge.

Once more I climbed up that ladder. Once more I inched shakily out to the edge. Once more my vision blurred, my stomach knotted up. But this time the jig was up. It was now or never. It was black or white. It's jump, or crawl home a loser.

I died inside. But then, in slow motion, now facing death at thirteen, I finally stepped off that terrifying edge.

It was a long swoop down. Much longer than I expected. And then I slammed into the water so hard the soles of my feet, which I didn't have pointed, practically burst open. I was shocked at how hard I hit. For the first time I understood how jumping off bridges could be the means to a successful suicide.

And so, it was done—

But, no. It hadn't been good enough. It had been, in fact, a bad jump. An inept jump. I could hear my horse master roaring "Get back up on zee haas!"

I went back up, faster this time, the soles of my feet tender and outraged. This time I jumped off with my arms held out like wings. I remembered to point my toes, but I left my arms stretched out. When I slammed into the water below, my under arms were seered, red and blistered.

So one more time, because it was still a mess of a jump, I raced back up the steps, the calls for the busses ringing out below. This really really was my last chance to get it right, to win a personal best.

I stood at the edge. Calm, now. Steel, now. I composed myself. I'd seen high divers do exactly this before they leapt out. I reminded myself to point my toes. I reminded myself to pull my arms in at the last moment. And above all, I asked myself to enjoy this moment of flying. Soar like a bird. Soar with freedom. Or, okay, fall like a dead bird. Fall like an avalanche. But do it with grace. Do it with awareness. Do it!

The last trumpet for the busses was sounded. I took a breath. I closed my eyes—
I stepped off the edge of the high dive platform—
And got it right.

Thirty years later I am again standing at the top of a high dive.

I'm standing at the top of the high dive at the Worthington Valley swim club in Baltimore, MD, to which I belong, and to which I bring my children every summer. I am standing at the top of this shortish high dive because I'm having a Mommy Machismo moment. I have made the bravado announcement to a small but worthy audience that I have no problem at all with jumping off the high dive. I've failed, however, to take into consideration that I am no longer thirteen years old, with the resilience of a thirteen year old in good shape after three punishing weeks of climbing mountains in Switzerland.

My audience consists of a six year old girl and an eight year old boy. They are otherwise known as my children, and they are, at this moment, staring up at me with such awestruck adoration, my mother heart is just about ready to burst.

But as I look down at them, I note that they are very very far away. Out of nowhere my stomach clenches, and my knees grow wobbly. I realize with a heart throbbing realization I have made an enormous error. I mean ginormous error. That there is no way my menopausal body is going to survive the plunge. It will crack and burst wide open the minute it touches that pretty aqua blue surface.

But I also realize that if I lose this moment of mother triumph and climb back down having chickened out, that wonderstruck look on my children's faces will disappear, and in its place will come disappointment, and they will no longer respect me. And that by the time they are hideous teenagers, when I will need any crumb of power I can find, they will dredge up this failure, and ignore everything I say.

So I must jump. It's as simple as that. The words carve their way through my brain. "Get back on zee haas!"

Go on. Get it over with. Quick, while nobody else is looking—

But now I note that all the other mothers and their children have noticed, and have gone silent as they stare up at me. Even the lifeguard is suddenly on alert. Oh no no no, I think, this is gonna be bad—

A cold chill clutches my heart, and I jump.

My children go scarlet with awe. As I hit the water I almost see the lifeguard leaping out of his chair. I plunge under the surface. I swear my ear drums burst. The top of my bathing suit rips off. My feet slam onto the cement bottom. But they still know how to react, those wonderful feet, because they push me back up to the surface—

So indeed, I do surface, gasping from the shock of it. Trying to maintain my cool, trying not to show shock and possible internal hemorrhaging, I attempt to set off for the side of the pool. But my arms have become tree trunks. My legs kick, feebly, but kick they do, so I do manage to get to the side. The steps are nowhere near, so I have to haul myself up and out of the pool like I used to be able to do…a long long time ago. I know it's not going to be pretty. I pray the lifeguard has the insight to stay away. I re-hook my top, smile blindly into nowhere, and with a silent curse, I suck in and manage to drag my shell-shocked body heavily out of the pool. My children, beside themselves with joy, are doing a jig by the side of the pool, so hopefully this gets in the way of a full view of my body flopping out like a beached whale onto the cement—

Only the sight of my children's thrilled faces, jumping up and down by the side of the pool, has kept me from drowning on the spot.

My Everests appear unexpectedly, in unexpected guises. They appear whether I want them or not. They don't take no for an answer. They are the biggest challenges in my life I've face so far. And they range from light to dark.

An Everest slipped in the day I clumsily fed my baby son his first solid food after months of carefree breastfeeding, and I suddenly realized that I had just been condemned to producing real meals, three times a day for the next eighteen years.

Another Everest was daring to remarry, after what I considered some very fine single living, even single parenting. I remarried, thereby creating a family of four mismatched children under the age of ten.

One Everest was letting go of alcohol forever.

One year my Everest was cradling my precious mother's body in my arms as my sisters and I dressed her minutes after her death, her head heavier than I could have imagined, lolling on my chest, right beside my heart. I thought of my infants asleep on this very same spot. Life and death, resting right on my heart. I couldn't breathe.

Everests are boarding planes and flying off into the unknown, alone. Everests are making new friends yet once again. Everests are standing up in front of a crowd and reading my work wondering if I'm feeling the love.

Everest is answering to "the man of the house" right after

my first divorce, wobbly and uncertain as to what my new societal designation was, and lighting up inside when I realized I meant it. "Man of the house." Yes. Me.

Everest is calling the friend I used to know, years after the falling out.

Everest is saying I'm sorry and not qualifying it with a 'but'.

When I was growing up, Edmund Hillary and his Sherpa Tenzing Norgay were in the background of conversations whirling around my head. Mt. Everest became a reality to me. It was the tallest mountain in the world, and these two men were the first to make it to the top and back down.

Ever since that camp in Switzerland, climbing mountains had struck me as an awesome endeavor. I admired those who had the passion for it. But climbing them was not for me. I was content to bask in the sight of those grand mountains. I was content to ski down their slopes. I was content to relish the amazing views, the scent of pine, the thin, crisp air. But climb them?

I still don't want to climb actual mountains.

But I do, however, climb the real life moments that stand in for Everest. That day I jumped off the high dive at Lake Geneva cleared out the debris of fear. It opened the door to the realization that being afraid didn't mean the answer was 'don't try' or 'don't act'.

Which is a fantastic thing.

Because here I sit, on the eve of my old age…okay, er… that sounds just too harsh…here I sit in the discernable future of my old age…much better…

Here I sit, stand, crawl, creek, soar, stumble, skip, and I can see the constant minor indignities that seem to accrue, but also the growing sense of a marvelously competent self with which to hold my own—

Old age is going to be one eye-opening and glorious Everest.

I'm…almost…looking forward to it.

The Wedding Dress

Wedding dresses are the #1 cause of divorce.

I will explain.

My wedding dress is cream velvet trimmed with amber. I see a euro-medieval flare to the full-length gown. I see a large graceful hood with intricate beading instead of a veil. I see long sleeves ending in more of the golden amber. I see suede boots, so feminine and embellished they hide the fact they are engineering marvels of comfort. I see, finally, a soft late winter evening, candle light and fragrant pine inside, falling snow and the magnificent Swiss Alps outside the huge windows of a wooden chalet.

I see, in fact, my third wedding. I see, to be precise, my third wedding dress. I see my glorious wedding dress dream. I can visit it any time. It is not lost to me. This keeps me alive and healthy and happy and free. I can still believe that dreams come true, over and over again.

Because I've had my deepest dream do so.

I've had two wedding dresses...so far. This does not make me a failure at marriage. This makes me a woman who knows how to keep a dream alive—

A very particular dream, a very woman-centric dream—

The Wedding Dress dream.

The fantasy, the chimera, that is the wedding dress. Not just any wedding dress. No. My very own wedding dress. The one I started fantasizing about at six.

My first wedding dress was a beauty that had fairytale Guinevere sleeves, all Belgian lace, which ended in a 'v' on my pristine nineteen year old hand, upon which was a baroque-inspired wedding ring, custom designed for me by a revered Laguna Beach, California jewelry designer.

My second wedding dress was Jil Sander. Architecturally simple cream wool maxi dress with a cashmere cream coat and long strands of pearls. The wedding band was plain gold, 18 carat. I was gaining two step-children as well as a new husband. Simple seemed the way to go.

I loved both wedding dresses equally. I floated down the aisle wearing the first one, and stepped confidently up to the justice of peace wearing the second.

I am smugly pleased, and yes, extremely relieved I've had two wedding dresses. I've beat the odds. I made Christmas last longer than one measly day. I have luxuriated in more than one measly wedding dress.

The general idea is that true love lasts forever. So that when she gets married to her one true love, she will never ever have another wedding. Hence the scores of elaborate first weddings. Since she knows, she just knows without a doubt he is the only man for her, she allows herself to plan a fabulous wedding. Her parents go along with her. But where her heart really lies, where most of her time and effort go, is into The Wedding Dress.

Because she's been thinking about it since she was six years old. That was when her own Aunt Nell got married, and walked, no, floated, down the church's rose petal strewn aisle, wearing the most amazing white gown, flowing out all around her. Aunt Nell wore a smile that looked like heaven. She looked like a ravishing angel. The six year old could only gaze dumbfounded and awe struck. Afraid to even speak to her normally fun-loving Aunt Nell. But later, asking her mother to tell her all about the whole day, she found out that this was what a wedding looked like. That everyone got to have one when they grew up and fell in love, just like Mommy and Daddy. Which meant, she slowly began to realize, her young heart starting to beat more rapidly, this meant such an amazing fate was to be hers as soon as she grew up and fell in love.

More stunningly, this meant that she too one day would be able to wear a gorgeous wedding dress. Such an amazingly awesome wedding dress. A wedding dress for a princess. That she too would get to become a ravishing angel, just like Aunt Nell. Mommy said so.

And so she had snuggled down in her bed, her mind just beginning the glorious journey it would take over the next twenty years, fantasizing about her own wonderful wedding, her own amazing wedding dress.

It would be her most psychologically nurturing dream.

We girls love and adore our wedding dress fantasies.

And fantasies are ours to keep. They are always there to offer nourishment, comfort, hope. They never end. Dreams are forever.

But let us look at the trajectory of this particular dream.

The thing is, a quiet misfortune begins to brew when the girl marries her one true love.

She has donned her most perfect wedding dress. She

has floated down the aisle, the most beautiful woman in the world. Then she danced heart out, twirling in that gorgeous creation. Her whole soul has been alight since she put it on that morning. Indeed, her whole being has been on fire since the fittings and shopping and deciding and choosing lace, ribbons, tulle, silk, brocade, velvet, and wedding showers and rings (the second most amazing dream, btw). Because it's happening. Her most amazing dream, her most loved dream, is coming true. She is a bride wearing the most beautiful wedding dress in the world.

But the moment she slips out of the most beautiful dress in the world, the one in which she was an absolute vision of radiance, the first touches of grief seep in, a certain hushed clamor of confused discontent. She moves into her new husband's waiting arms—

And out of her warm, cozy and deeply comforting dream. She moves out of the dream forever.

Now?

She has to take her most beautiful fantasy to the dry-cleaners so they can do whatever they do to preserve it. It will then come back to her in a large white box that is to remain unopened in order to preserve it, and she will never ever see her gorgeous dress again. The dress she has dreamed about since she was six.

This is bad. Don't kid yourself, mothers and fathers who've paid for the wedding dress. Or innocent husbands who, I understand have shaky, newly married issues of their own. There is grief, an open wound in that little girl, now grown woman, who has just seen the end of her biggest, most dreamy, and indeed most comforting fantasy. This luscious world is dead. Finito. It can never ever be lived again—

Unless…

I hasten to say this 'unless' is absolutely *not* the first thing on her mind. She's not looking for solutions to her wedding dress loss. She's accepting it like the loss of a beloved pet.

No, the obvious solution to her wedding dress loss doesn't begin to rise up until the marriage begins to rain down its inevitable difficulties—

Of course the solution also never appears in any specificity.

Instead it lurks deep down, just waiting for that moment to live again.

So the marriage begins to pile up its usual mess of issues, and one day the word 'divorce' pops into her mind. Such is the power of the lurking wedding dress dream, the pilot light that never goes out, that word 'divorce' begins to croon and whisper in her ear. She's still not aware that the wound of the lost dream is struggling to gain life again. But it is, and it knows how much she misses it, how much she craves it, how much she doesn't even know how much she misses and craves it.

It is a fact of life. She craves the euphoria of her wedding dress dream like a drug. Therefore the dream struggles to gain footing as her marriage founders.

And so it happens. Weakened by those lost dreams, she finds herself slowly but surely wending her way to divorce.

Soon, although not right away, because divorce grief must play out, her subconscious will align with the inevitable realization. It's subtle, this shift. She barely knows when or why. All she knows is that one night, lying in bed, seemingly out of nowhere, her inner child rises up and remembers her beloved wedding dress dream.

It will take a moment. First she'll remember Aunt Nell walking down the aisle. She will remember her mother's arms around her telling her all about weddings and wedding dresses. And then? Then, yes, she finally realizes that The Wedding Dress Dream can be hers again. It bursts forth in triumph. Euphoria suffuses her so completely, it almost throws her out of bed.

She lies there in new bliss (and a slight sweat), thinking visions of tulle and lace, and already designing and smiling in the dark so hard her cheeks hurt. After awhile she'll fall asleep and sleep like a baby for the first time in months.

The wedding dress is the dark, unspoken malingerer behind every divorce.

No one wants to admit this.

But it is true.

The death of the Wedding Dress Dream is the most under-acknowledged cause of divorce today.

Upon getting married, this issue should be dealt with promptly and thoroughly.

But it isn't.

Personally, I am at one with that, up here in the Swiss Alps, draped in velvet and crystal, in front of candlelight and snowflakes—

Dancing in my third wedding dress dream.

Cooking for the
Ones You Love

I am a woman who, like trillions of women, has raised a few children, a couple of husbands, and several pets. As a result of tending to their needs, I have spent years in the kitchen cooking full on healthy, nutritionally balanced and creative meals for them.

In addition to those meals, I've spent years making lunches for children to take to school, prepared before I'd even had my first sip of coffee. I've put together perfect snacks for the hungry college student home for the holidays, the whimpering three year old, the despairing husband, and the cat (she liked whipped cream). I've gone through a baking phase, producing chocolate cakes, butterscotch cookies, lemon meringue pies, rhubarb cobbler and Turkish cupcakes…at midnight. I've helped the teenage daughter adjust her starvation diet before the prom to help her actually lose weight. I have adjusted my own diet to accommodate things like pregnancies, root canals, and cross-country moves. I've enticed suspicious kitties to ignore the medicine lurking in their food dish. And I have done this three times a day, day in and day out, for a long long time.

So you see, I am done, so very done.

I cannot look a pot in the face these days. I cannot bear to make a peanut butter sandwich, cut in fours, crust off, even if the recipient is a pint-sized visitor. I will not stir a drink or slice a pear or dice a tomato or measure a cup of sugar, even for the new neighbor standing at my back door, empty cup in hand. I will not get out the blender or beat the eggs or set the timer or clean up the kitchen counter.

I will not scoop out a dish of ice cream or blend ricotta and tomato sauce. I will not stack a lasagna, will not sauté zucchini or wash blueberries. I won't fry A-one prime meat. I won't bake honey and lime chicken. I won't cut out a three-page recipe. I won't look at a food magazine.

Do not give me a cookbook, no matter how pretty the pictures are. Particularly don't give me any of the classic cookbooks. I got all those for my first marriage. My first husband took them with him in the divorce, and I don't care.

Don't offer me a new stove, six burners, gas, stainless steel, unless said stove comes with an attached chef.

Don't offer me quartz or marble counter tops for the kitchen to lure me in. I can't be fooled. No TV or stereo will lure me in either. No charming set of milk glass, even though last year I made the mistake of announcing I was starting to collect the stuff. I'll explain later the difference between collecting things and cooking.

I cannot do grocery stores anymore.

I cannot go down another aisle, pulling out English Muffins and Pringles…asking myself why English muffins and Pringles are even on the same aisle. And as this questions pounds on my brain each and every time I go into the grocery store, surely you understand my pain.

I cannot walk down the frozen food aisle anymore. Beside

the fact it is way too cold (am I the only one who wears a scarf to the grocery store?) I now have painful flashbacks of the way it was—

I am back in a grocery store, in the days of yore, choosing ice cream for a family of six, which necessitated six flavors, but not vanilla anymore, because one of them, I forget which one, had moved on. I think it was the three year old. She hadn't figured out what flavor she'd moved on to, but she sure as heck was over vanilla.

The flashback continues down the next aisle, where the beans for the chili and the canned tomatoes were stacked. Just toss a few of each in the cart? No, because the oldest boy...the only boy actually, and I'm afraid that had gone to his head, now insisted that tomato paste added a certain je ne sais quoi to the chili, so would I please commence to add it to the family recipe?

And thirteen year old princess over there, still into apple scented shampoo, the kind that permeated the house, the garage, and the interior of every car we owned, Princess had newly discovered that vegetables were edible cooked to death in a stew. So she wanted to know if I would add some green pepper to the same chili in which the son now wanted tomato paste? And then there was the husband—there was still a husband in this flash back—wanted me to chop up the tomato *before* I added the beans because the beans would get chopped into mush if they were chopped at the same time as the tomatoes were being chopped, and surely I know how much he hated mush.

To his credit, he asked this favor of me nervously because he knew how I was feeling about the kitchen and everything to do with it.

Speaking of husbands. I've had two. Both wonderful in their own way. And both becoming excellent cooks by virtue of the fact they started cooking more and more as I began cooking less and less.

With the first husband it was more happenstance than planned. We arrived at our cohabitation, age nineteen and twenty respectively, without either of us knowing how to cook. Both of our mothers were exceptional cooks, and so busy in general, it was simply easier to do all the cooking themselves. Frankly, when I got married at nineteen, fresh from my parents' house, not only couldn't I cook, I didn't know how to clean a bathroom or hang up my clothes. For some reason I did know how to iron. And how to sew.

My first husband fell into love of cooking because we watched a tv show called "Galloping Gourmet", which came on just as we got home from classes and were starving. I watched it for fun. My husband watched it like he had just discovered manna from heaven. And soon, once a week, he was making one of the recipes. The first "Chicken Grismelda", a soggy mess of chicken, blue cheese, spinach and thyme was so good, it amazed even us. For a time then, I watched my husband cook, and praised him lavishly. I didn't hate cooking at that stage. But it didn't thrill me. I was happy to be the cheerleader.

Being college kids, though, and undisciplined at best, real cooking was sporadic, and ultimately fell into my hands as our lives dutifully progressed to jobs, houses and children.

There was no way I could avoid that.

But I grew weary. Very weary.

Luckily, and in the time honored scheme of things, my children did grow up and basically leave home.

Thus began the years in which I did not have to cook

as religiously. I realize now these years began the years of Teaching the Husband to Cook. And as this is one of those good things that deserves to be shared, I will do so now.

Here is How To Teach The Husband How To Cook:

Begin by slowly cooking less.

Very slowly.

This is most effective if you are a good cook to begin with, and have been feeding your husband lavishly for years. This includes such luxuries as knowing just what he's in the mood for at all times, whether it's breakfast, a snack while watching basketball, or that special dessert on Wednesday nights to help get through the rest of the week.

You start by *not* cooking dinner a couple of times in *one* week. You get take-out instead. At first this will seem novel—MacDonald's at home, just you two, candles lit. (Remember, the kids are gone by this time. There's no quitting cooking while they are still home. You know it. I know it. They know it.). An evening of Chinese take-out of those boxes, out on the deck. Dunkin Donuts on tv trays in bed for that early night in.

But the well-fed husband will soon not want take-out. Next time you bring up take-out, he'll look sad. You wait this out. Then, if he's a real man and therefore craving real food, he'll cautiously suggest he cook that night. You must look skeptical. So, immediately defensive, he'll say it's not like he doesn't know his way around the kitchen. After all, it's his kitchen too, he'll say. And there were those times when he was forced to do the cooking. Like when you had a new baby. Or your girls' nights out. Or that time you left him to go to London for ten days, leaving him home alone with four kids.

And slowly you allow him to convince you. You come to

see that maybe he does know his way around his very own kitchen. So that, okay. He can cook dinner that night, if he really wants to.

And so he does.

And the process has begun.

Next step—*never* fuss about what he brings home from the grocery store. He's going into that awful place, right? He is not suffering from PTSD from years of living in the grocery store. It's not that big of a deal for him to get the groceries. So, never berate. No matter what he brings home. If you berate, going to the grocery store will become less attractive to your sweet husband. You do *not* want that to happen.

Number three? You must be willing to help with the dishes afterwards, but only after you've introduced him to the art of Cleaning Up As He Goes Along.

Eventually, you will be a woman about it, and begin doing the dishes every time. After all, you didn't have to go to the grocery store or cook for…what is it now? Three weeks? Isn't it amazing how time flies when you aren't…cooking?

But I reiterate, you do the dishes every time he cooks. And only beginning this after you've showed him how to clean up as he goes along.

You must proceed with caution and delicacy. Because who in their right minds will love realizing they are being trained to wash the dishes…in any shape or form.

This is tricky because cleaning up as you go along is actually *advanced* cooking.

Mothers, you are already so accomplished at this, that I feel a gentle reminder is necessary. It is most likely you clean up as you go along without even noticing you're doing it. This beautiful habit evolves from necessity. Keeping the workspace cleaned up as one goes along preparing a meal creates more space in which to work. It allows for one's organizational abilities to flourish. No hysterical hunting for the most important ingredient, pan, utensil or cheese grater. Being organized means actually being able to remember to heat the plates—a task which would be lost in the chaos of a meal that isn't being swept clean every step of the way. In my house, if Mom forgot this step, my sweet Dad would... well, I don't know what, because by the time I became aware of the purity of warmed up dinner plates, Mom never forgot. My first husband loved this and never forgot. My second husband, though, thought it superfluous...until he began cooking and it was his own hard won meal began going onto those ice cold plates. Then he finally understood the good of a heated dinner plate.

But, the man in your life is new to this concept. They have no reference of experience unless they've done their own cooking in the past, which is not likely if you are reading this with any interest at all.

So, you will need to be patient in this process. Remember there is much anxiety for the new chef, therefore he really does, at the very beginning, have too much on his mind to handle Cleaning Up As He Goes Along.

The process of your beloved person taking over your kitchen duties is a slow one. I'd give it a year. A year in which he is given more and more responsibility in barely perceptible amounts. It's obviously best if he doesn't realize this is happening. It is even more desirable that he perceive himself as having a good time. That is why you present the more onerous tasks slowly.

But yes. Give it at least a year. He needs to be guided lovingly, most lovingly, for instance, through each holiday.

These are big. These are scary. These often involve feeding a whole heck of a lot more people than he is used to feeding.

These meals also have to be accomplished with a modicum of sobriety. Probably total abstinence from viewing the sport showing on tv. Maybe all bets will be off for Super Bowl, and you'll just have to man up and cook those nachos and chili dogs and buy those beers yourself. But as to the other holidays? Sports are always lurking. There's basketball around Easter. Baseball, which now runs all year, is certainly on for Fourth of July. Add to tennis and golf playing every Sunday, cooking on Sunday may in the end prove to be your most difficult hurdle.

So again, loving patience, one game at a time, one Sunday at a time, is what is needed to fully integrate your man into his new role as chef.

Remember, that although you are so done with cooking and grocery shopping, he isn't. He couldn't be. You've been doing it for him. So to him, if you've gradually handed over those reins to him without him noticing, he'll only know he's now having so much fun cooking. Cooking is his new, pleasurable hobby.

Some women are going to inevitably have trouble letting go. Even though they hate it so much. This is a classic control issue. Housewives specifically and women in general, have a huge problem with this when it comes to the running of their homes. They…we, truly know we like it done our way. We want all the plaudits, although we no longer want the work.

Let me present this thought. If your beloved starts cooking now, he could never end up cooking more than you did, particularly if you add the million and two school lunches and snacks you made. And he certainly will never be as a good of a cook as you were/are. And he'll never ever get the snacks right-

Or maybe he will. Can you/me accept this? Can you/me thrive on this new freedom?

You're doing your man a favor. You are adding to his repertoire of accomplishments. How many men out there adore a good meal, but are afraid to try. Afraid yes. But not unwilling. He's just inhibited. All grown-up inhibited. You are releasing him from the pain of fear of trying something he thinks he can only dream about. Especially as you are now feeding him less and less satisfactorily...

This brings me to the last important detail.

From the very beginning, absolutely rave over his food. Eat every speck on the plate, go back for more, and lick your plate clean.

Believe me, soon this will not be an act.

He will get really good at this cooking game. Really good.

Because afterall, he has been taught by the master herself.

My Traffic Cops

I am a type A jerk of a driver.

I believe in cutting you off, and blowing the horn if you are texting when the light turns green. My lip curls if your car says 'careful, baby on board.' Because why am *I* the one who has to be careful about *your* baby? I avert my eyes at the sight of white mini vans, and most especially at the big white mini van in front of me at a red light. My heart sinks, because I know without a doubt the person driving this car, the person who actually went out of his way to buy a car that looks like a bath tub, is in no hurry to get anywhere. So that when the light turns green, he will seem to have all kinds of doubt as to whether or not he actually wishes to move forward.

I sneer at Hummer drivers for a different reason entirely. These drivers aren't idiots or pudgy or weak. These owners are class A jerks, and they want you to know it. So I sneer because I know I am a better jerk than they are. It's organic to sneer at Hummer drivers.

I have no patience for the elderly driver who is "cautious", or more to the point, oblivious. They should be removed from the road years before politer society deems it necessary. Before they hurt someone. Polite society is afraid of appearing harsh to this delicate segment of society. I feel being polite to the elderly is demeaning to them. And worrisome for the rest of the population. The day I saw my father sail through a red light and deny it later, was the day decisions were made to permanently separate him from his car.

I am amused at how fast Prius drivers are. How they cut into traffic even more belligerently than I do. This is obviously because they are, down inside, deeply ashamed of wearing their current brand of PC on their sleeve, the sleeve they now have to wear to cover up the tattoos of dripping blood from smoking guns they got before they became so ecologically minded.

Yes. I am a type A driver.

But I am, in my advanced age, trying not to be a Type A driver. I am trying to become a better driver. A more polite driver.

Particularly when it comes to my bêtes noirs, traffic cops.

It was specifically because I wasn't polite enough…or polite at all, to the cop invading my space, that got me ordered out of my car and made to perform a sobriety test, twelve years after my last drink. You try passing a drunk driving test while self-righteously enraged, wearing stilettos, and having just consumed a huge meal that included copious amounts of garlic which the younger cop kept insisting smelled like alcohol, shrilling out in a high pitched voice "I can smell it from here."

After putting me through my paces, they told me I failed, at which point, knowing without a doubt my last drink had been a weak gin and tonic consumed, like I said, twelve years before, I demanded to be given a breathalyzer test. "You sure about that, ma'am?" said the older cop, steel in his voice, cold-staring me like I stood there with a bloodied knife and a corpse at my feet. Oh yeah, baby, I was sure. Go on. Make me blow!

He didn't. I was sent on my way, after being endorsed to 'drive carefully now'.

I don't like cops. Traffic cops, specifically.

But, more inconveniently, they don't like me.

It all started the day I got my driver's license, the very second I turned sixteen.

I leapt into my new (hand-me-down) car and headed out.

I was reveling in my adulthood, testing out the Pasadena freeway, when a cop pulled me over. Just because I changed lanes right in front of him? Hey! I was lost. I was nervous. I'd never driven on the freeway before, and it was the Pasadena Freeway, and the freeway was falling apart, with no such things as on-ramps being where they were supposed to be.

After showing me off the freeway to a side street, he showed up at my window and said "Driver's license, please." I had to pull out my wet-behind-the-ears paper version of the license I would soon get in the mail. His eyebrows rose up. Even I could see the suppressed amusement. He cleared his throat. Asked me why I thought he pulled me over. I, huffily, said I didn't know. He said because I had changed lanes right in front of him without signaling. I was completely surprised. I'd been having enough trouble trying to get in front of him, without *also* having to use my signal at the same time. What did he want from me?

He didn't give me a ticket, but he issued me a warning. "Better get more practice with someone who *really* knows how to drive, young lady."

That parting shot burned into my soul. The hair rose up

on my neck, and I wanted to whip my car around…which is to say feint and punt, trying to make sure to use my blinker whenever was needed, back and forth, back and forth, all the way around, to tell him he was a total jerk and that he didn't know what he was talking about. That I was a superb driver. That it had been the Pasadena Freeway's fault, and he should go away and bother someone who really deserved to have their ego crushed.

This event, occurring on the very day I got my driver's license, heralded (although I didn't know it at the time) a life that has included, like the cold that keeps coming back, traffic cops. It heralded a life of being pulled over by a cop here, by a cop there, by a cop every where. Pasadena, Chicago, Evanston, Ponte Vedra and Jacksonville, FL, Baltimore Md, and So Cal.

Traffic cops. Motorcycle cops. Highway patrol cops. They all think they have the right to pull me over and give me a ticket. I went to Catholic school. I know right from wrong. Who do these guys (and occasional girl) think they are?

I've been pulled over for speeding (42 in a 35), driving without a taillight, changing lanes without signaling, more speeding, and more speeding still. In my defense about the speeding, I've never gotten a ticket for speeding on the freeway…no wait a minute, yes I have. But that time was because I'd had a wart removed from my eyelid and the eye was stinging and watering and I could barely see and was rushing home so I could pop a mountain of Tylenol. In fact the cop almost wouldn't let me drive home, so concerned was he I might run into someone. I sort of think he should have called an ambulance for me, instead of taking all that time to write me the ticket.

My relationship with traffic cops is so bad that I have even gotten not one but two tickets for jay walking. Jay walking? As if simply by walking I'm a threat to public safety? What about the clown who's driving down the freeway at forty-five miles an hour? What about the jerk who's riding his bike at night, wearing headsets, with no blinking light on the back of his non street-worthy vehicle?

One time a young cop pulled me over for speeding on the Florida Intercoastal (I was on my way to therapy. Give me a break!), and during the course of checking my driver's license, writing the ticket, and having me sign it, the wind caught my driver's license and blew it away. Forever. His hardcore demeanor waivered, and for a second I saw a little boy in trouble with Mom, but in the nick of time, he reverted to a cop who is never wrong, and handed me my ticket. And let me get another driver's license all by myself.

I once got five tickets in one month. The month was May. I was nineteen. And I was driving my boyfriend's Porsche. Three of the tickets were for the broken rear taillight. Two were from the same cop. I knew what he really wanted was a closer look at my sexy little car. Not the pissed-off sexy babe driving it.

I once got a ticket the afternoon of the morning I'd just been to court to pay another ticket. That one almost caused my stalwart second husband to weep.

I got a ticket for having an out of date registration on my license plate. I was going through a divorce, so less pulled together than I would normally be about such matters. I had two children under the age of two. My three-month old daughter began to scream from her car seat. So I got out of my car, walked back to the cop, who was taking his sweet time with the ticket, and asked, due to the screaming baby, if he would hurry things up a little. I didn't think my tone of voice showed what I really thought about him. But his head whipped up like a cobra about to strike. "Okay, ma'am, I remember now. You were speeding. I have to write you up for that too." My daughter continued to scream, and I prayed every night for two weeks that he would go on to be the father of several colicky babies.

There was the time I received a letter from the state of California. It read, "Dear Ms. Yunker. We are worried about you." It was almost enough to warm the cockles of my stone cold heart. They went on to say that the proliferation of traffic tickets I was getting seemed to suggest I was unhappy and maybe needed help. Had I considered getting help? Because, they needed to pleasantly remind me, if I got any more tickets they would have to separate me from my driver's license. And if that happened they felt sure my peace of mind would be even more seriously compromised than it already seemed to be.

In real life I'm on the straight-laced side. My cleavage is polite and subdued. I am the stick in the mud, the non-drinker, in a crowd of loud partiers. I'm the cautious one who never falls into the pool with my clothes on. I don't think practical jokes are funny. Halloween costumes either. I'm the rule follower, except during my pot smoking days. At the airport? I am one of those who actually does get there two hours before the flight. Extra baggage already paid for.

I always figured that eventually I'd get old enough to either become a type B driver, or venerable enough that cops would simply leave me alone. But that didn't happen. I can't seem to manage to become a type B driver, and so they don't leave me alone.

Now traffic cops are younger than my son, which makes

me want to burst into tears, but that only worked once for me. I was twenty-two, or some adorable age like that. I was driving the husband's sexy little Porsche and had just moved to Chicago. I was lost. So when the cute cop pulled me over, I simply burst into very real tears, and he gallantly waved me and my snazzy little Porsche on.

No more, honey.

No cop is entranced with the middle-aged woman. I never thought of this. I always thought age would add a certain gravitas to how the traffic cop treated me when he pulled me over. But no. I either remind him of his wife or his mother. Both scenarios can be fraught with peril.

All I know now is I am too old to be pulled over anymore. I am too mature. I have my blond hair, and I have my pride. And I can let go of the bad girl behind the wheel of a car.

So, I've slowed it down, baby. I am taking different actions.

I leave earlier than is my wont, so that I'm not the raving maniac on the road who's late, again.

I've cut back on coffee.

I got an SUV. This has slowed me down because these babies just won't be whipped around like an acrobat.

And I haven't gotten a ticket in four years. This is a personal best.

But I don't want to jinx it—

Let us never speak of this matter again.

Telling Our Daughters About the Facelift

I'm not afraid of cops. Or rollercoasters. Or arguing with someone taller than me. But I am afraid of my grown-up daughter. Not all the time. Or even most of the time. But when it *is* one of those times, then yes, I'm afraid of my daughter.

Like telling her about the facelift.

Have you had this experience yet? The one in which you want a facelift, so you cautiously bring it up to your grown daughter?

Did the idea go over well with her? No it didn't, did it. She was appalled, right?

"You have no reason to get a facelift, Mom," she said, her voice instantly rising. "You're supposed to age naturally. Didn't you teach me that? Besides, you don't need one."

According to our daughters' pristine ideals we are to be at one with every single bit of our crumbling body and face. We are to spend that money on something, anything, else. Or better yet, not spend it at all, because we realize what a pointless luxury it is…and oh my, we don't want to be accused of pointless luxury, do we? Into which category a facelift most definitely falls.

Do you have a daughter like that? The kind who has a twenty-five year old's face, because, well, she *is* twenty-five? But still feels it's her right to council you against having a facelift? So that you, well certainly me, replies with as much hauteur as I can muster, given the obvious condition of my face, "when you are my age you will understand."

"Not me," said my daughter, confidently. And obliviously…in my oh so humble opinion. "It's because you live in Southern California," she said, warming to her subject. "You've gotten messed up by their skewed ideals about how a woman should look," said my Oregon resident daughter.

Actually, it wasn't Southern California that skewed my brain. No. It was my addiction to fashion magazines. Which started early, so that by age nineteen I knew absolutely I would avail myself to plastic surgery "when the time came".

I am the first to admit that my addiction to high fashion magazines like Vogue and Bazaar (which I also get in three other languages) is a sin I have perpetrated on myself. The sin of gazing upon the visages of perpetual twenty-year olds as I leave twenty years old farther and farther behind. So far behind it has become invisible.

My sister-in-law says the same thing happens when one teaches college. She says when she first started teaching she could hold her own. She wasn't that much older than her students. But as the years rolled by, it became harder and harder not to notice how they stayed dewy-skinned, while she became more and more beaten up.

So no, SoCal hasn't forced me to have an addiction to keeping up with twenty year old faces. Fashion magazines are the culprit, if there is a need to blame something for wanting a facelift.

But just as I keep my weight in check, and wash my hair, and iron my clothes, I have a vested interest in my face. It's the one that greets me every morning. So when the aging process moved past my comfort zone, and I knew there was something I could do about it, I did.

There's always the photo that does the deciding for you. It's the one in which, at the time, you thought you looked awesome, if you did say so yourself. But when you finally look at the picture closely, you see that you look exactly like your mother did when she first started talking about a face-lift. She never went on to get one…but this is where you are stronger than your mother was—

In spite of your daughter.

Getting started is just as easy as making an appointment for a mammogram…I know. Not easy. But you do, because you are a strong woman with a desire to be good to your body…in every way. So with the face lift, you gird your loins and call up three plastic surgeons, making an appoint-ment with each for a consultation. A free consultation.

You walk out of each consultation lighter than air, be-cause the plastic surgeon seemed to know you intimately. He knew exactly what you wanted. You didn't even have to explain yourself twice. He knew. He just knew.

He's going to restore your precious face to a facsimile of what it used to be. And just like that, you have found the doctor of your dreams.

This is an honest, indeed organic and holistic, and even spiritual journey you are on. Because you're not trying to fool people about your age. You just want to look how you feel inside. My grandmother used to tell me, "Every morning I get up and am shocked all over again at the face I see in the mirror. It isn't at all how I feel inside."

The ones who say you should work on acceptance of the way things are should just drink from their sippy cups and come back later when they can relate.

The ones who tell you you're crazy, that you look perfect, well, these people love you. They truly love you, so that what you actually look likes makes no difference to them. You look like you. Like gazing at my mother when she would say "Should I get a facelift?" And even though I thought that if she wanted to then she should, I didn't see an older face. I just saw the beloved face of my mother.

Then there are those who immediately fly into a blood curdling narrative of plastic surgery mistakes. You have the answer ready—those women wanted too much done. You are not like those women. Your lips will not swell to tsunami size, nor will you have that awful wind tunnel thing. Plastic surgeons don't do that anymore. Your cheeks will not turn into chipmunks. Your facelift will look natural. "Hah," sniff the disaster friends.

You sniff back. They are jealous, therefore to be pitied.

Besides, you're nervous about it already. Why can't they just be supportive?

Finally then, there are our daughters.

We want our daughters' approval and indeed admiration, more than we want the love of a good man. But it is so easy to go wrong with our daughters, particularly when they've grown up and know it all. Particularly when in some subliminal way they are just like us, only they are stronger now in their beliefs because they haven't been tested. They haven't been beaten down by life like we have, hence the desire (may I even say need?) for a facelift, thank you very much.

Our daughters are our biggest hurdle. They are the ones we are actually cowed by. This is because we used to be God to them. We used to be the most beautiful, the smartest, the most incredibly perfect Mom to them. And we loved that. Am I right?

But one day we were no longer these things to them. One day it all changed. They grew up, and now, only too often, they think they know better than us about so many things.

Their only too predictable scathing reaction will still hurt. The daughter is inflamed because even though she's willing to see it her mother's way, that maybe she is looking a little um…older, well isn't that life? Isn't it simply more honest to age gracefully? What about all those other fine ways of being you taught her way back when she was little and you still looked fabulous. Have you forgotten all that? Now instead, you're telling her you are going to do something completely narcissistic. This is so appalling to her on so many levels she falls back into a childish temper tantrum.

She doesn't want you to change. She doesn't want to be reminded you are indeed getting older. She wants only to think of you as her Mom, steadfast and true.

But go forward with strong heart and good will. You will be so glad you did it. And one day, your precious baby will come around.

The day my highly loving but often dictatorial daughter caved and asked me to whom she should go for Botox was the day I knew the playing ground was beginning to be leveled. She was by now thirty-three and a stressed out lawyer. But she was younger by far than when I started Botox…

Did I argue with her?

Oh no. I took her to her first Botox appointment.
We went out for lunch afterwards.
And had dessert too.

So if you are considering a facelift, do not waver.
Just get the hurdle of your daughter over with first.
Have faith. She will become your biggest ally in the end.
Which is what every mother wants, right?
In addition to a face that more closely resembles the one you had when she was fifteen.

Bathing Suit and the Gym

One day the sun came up and without warning I tripped over yet another step in the aging process—

It's never going to end.

Am I right?

But this step was liberating. This step made me happy. Even though PC speaking, I was not supposed to be happy about it.

Because I'm supposed to be that marvelous woman who doesn't care what other people think about me. I'm supposed to be the woman who honestly believes that no one is paying any attention to me at all, and in particular, you see, when I'm wearing a bathing suit.

Is there an actual real live woman out there who doesn't care what she looks like in a bathing suit out on a glaring beach, or in a hot tub full of twenty-somethings, or at a cool pool party where even the women her age look good in a bathing suit…and she doesn't?

The liberating step I took?

I gave up bathing suits.

More precisely, because I am stronger in my aging process than I often let on, I started saying no to activities that required the wearing of a bathing suit. And I said no without lying.

"I'm sorry. I don't do hot tubs anymore. Can't bear to put on a bathing suit."

"I think I'll pass on the beach today. Too self-conscious to wear a bathing suit in public anymore.

"No I don't want to go to the Cayman Islands and scuba dive. Bathing suits, ya know." Although in the case of the Cayman Islands, it was really because I am terrified of scuba diving.

I like…no…I *love* having gotten to the point where I can say "I am *not* putting on a fucking bathing suit" without even the hint of a chagrined blush. Usually this blunt display of vulnerability shuts the do-gooders and earnest people right up.

I used to love swimming. I used to love putting on my bikini and tanning. I used to be at one with the public display of my youthful body in a bathing suit on the shockingly bright beaches of Southern California.

Buying the yearly bikini, back in the days when I *had* the task of buying a yearly bikini, was a very big deal. Back then we bought one bathing suit. We did not buy sixteen like they do now.

The reason for owning one bathing suit at a time was the tan line. The one that came into its own after we took the bikini off. In order to have that pristine tan line, the bathing suit lines had to be uniform. Which meant sticking to one bathing suit. By the end of the summer, the bikini was shredded. It was a washed out version of its original glory. But our tans? They were gorgeous.

My best bikini was deep yellow, which I wore down to the thread. It saw me through my high school graduation trip to Hawaii—

I doubt my parents actually felt I deserved a graduation present of that magnitude after a distinctly lackluster trip through my school years. But my best friend told me she was going to Hawaii for her graduation present and did I want to go too?

Next thing I knew I was in Hawaii with my soon-to-be ex best friend, for three weeks of stress and arguing, and that yellow bikini. And even though our friendship did not survive the trip (it was all her fault…no really, *all her fault…*), the yellow bikini did. Frayed, but alive.

Today, even though I am blunt on the subject of my disinterest in good times requiring a bathing suit, I actually own two bathing suits. Yes. But I haven't worn them in three years. I bought them because I was going to swim in the saltwater pool at the fancy gym I joined. I was going to swim because my back was killing me, and I was sure swimming would be better than jogging, or even yoga.

Before I settled on going to a gym to swim, starting to swim in general was the plan.

So I ran the idea passed my friends. Naturally my friends had a lot of advice. Given how far off the advice proved to be, I wondered how well my friends actually knew me, which led to my wondering if they were truly friends, and if, in fact, I had any true friends, which lead me to notice that my supply of friends was dwindling, which lead to…but I digress.

My purist yoga friends suggested swimming in the ocean. The frigid Pacific Ocean, just after dawn. Organic and all that. Smugly loving the rigor in their daily life and all. Suggesting that being at one with the awesomeness of the ocean was simply the most life-affirming thing one could ever do. Would I like to join them on their oh so amazing, 6:00 am swims in the ocean?

Where is the emoticon for horror?

"No thank you," I said. "I'll only hold you joyful people back."

Then there was the group of friends who still had teenagers at home. These friends were in practical, get-it-done mode. They suggested I go to the local YMCA and swim. It's cheap, they said enthusiastically.

Listen, telling me something is cheap doesn't work. Not that I don't like a bargain. When Loehmann's was still in business, I got my most beautiful clothing from there and loved every minute of the deal.

But cheap connected with the local YMCA? It morphed right into a low rent, possibly not too clean, rundown, indoor pool filled with hyped up school kids peeing in it because they thought it was funny.

There was also the issue of chlorine when it came to pools. Chlorine and my blond hair. Which might turn green in a chlorine pool. I ran crying to my hairdresser. He said he *didn't think* my hair would turn green because the processes were so mild now, and in fact, bleach wasn't even used anymore. But, the coward wouldn't commit to an absolute green light.

So, the idea nearly died the chlorine day. But then another friend, a good friend this one, pointed out that there were salt-water swimming pools. Salt-water pools would not hurt my hair, said the friend. And might even give me the idea I was swimming in the wonderful, oh so natural, ocean.

So I Googled 'public salt water pools', and found Equinox Gyms.

Equinox gyms, it turned out, had everything. They had fancy spas facilities in addition to the miracle making machines.

Equinox Gyms were nation wide, the latest thing in gyms. They indeed had salt-water pools. They were expensive.

Never mind about money, I thought, hope rising. My personal well-being was at stake here. This was caring for my aging and weary body. This was me, a more than grown woman, a woman who was old enough to have grand children if my children had just once in their lives followed the established way of doing things.

This was me, a woman who could almost afford the best gym in town.

I've periodically joined gyms. I prefer ballet, jogging, and yoga—the solitary sport that requires only one's body, and perhaps a teacher or two, to get down to business and sweat. But these sports never addressed the muscle tone the way those grandiose machines in gyms do. Hence the need for the occasional gym membership.

But I don't like them. The grunting. The threat of road rage. I mean machine rage. The noise. The clangs and snorts, the pounding music. The fight for a spot on the stairmaster things. The lusty, sweaty, unconcealed competitiveness. The need to wear eye make-up…

But I always went for awhile because those machines did do awesome things for my muscles, when I was still at an age that a few weeks here and there at the gym sorted out the toned muscle issue very well.

Where am I…
Swimming. Bodies in bathing suits. Back problems.
Desperation.
I got to work, researching salt water pools and Equinox gyms.

So the day comes that I enter the Equinox gym closest to me. This is as traumatic as going to the airport. Especially for those folk who are my age, and I do include the older men coming in too. It's not for the faint-hearted or the world-weary. Or for the one on one mission and one mission only, to sign up for their great big salt water pool and swim in it. You are not interested in the machines.

It turns out you will not be shown the pool right off. No.

Upon entering the gym you will be accosted by Matt, Kim, Amber, Tony, Jackie, Bob, Bill and Barry. They bounce up to you, eyes bright, huge smiles on their faces, all so very eager to help you with whatever you may need. They are wearing gym clothes. They are wearing pony-tails. They are lightly tanned. They are all in excellent shape. The kind of shape you used to be in—

They are twenty-six.

And they're all yours. What can they help you with? The pool, you say. You say you want to swim in the salt water pool here at Equinox. You say this in a whispered garble because you've forgotten all gym lingo the minute you switched over to yoga, ten years ago, where nobody bounces, nobody wears pony tails, but where they say things like 'Namaste' and 'Breeeeeathe'.

The fact is, I found out one cannot enter a gym just to use the pool. This would be just too much for Matt, Kim, Amber, Tony, Jackie, Bob, Bill and Barry. They are not going to let that happen.

Because they are unquellable in their conviction that what you want, in your heart of hearts, is their body. And they truly believe, in their innocence, that they can give exactly that to you. But that this miracle will not even begin to happen by swimming, for god sake, in their salt water pool.

Of course you would love to be as buff as they are, but you are now wise enough to know it is not possible. Especially as you've already wrecked your body over the past fifty years attempting that particular rebirth and maintenance, in Ashtanga yoga, running five miles a day, riding horses, Zumba, Jazzercize and even ballet itself, to mention a few roads down which your body has gone. Hence the present need for a swimming pool.

So that now all you want to do at their gym is to swim. And you are prepared to spend the big bucks to do so.

You'd think they'd been told by corporate to give the customer what the customer wants.

But no. Not this crew. Maybe they see in you their own mothers, whom they love very much. And whom they would dearly love to help get into shape. In the end it doesn't matter because they are going to take you on a tour of the gym whether you like it or not.

And since you can smell the barely dried scent of Mommy love dust feathered all over their shiny ponytails and perfectly straightened teeth, and in your heart-of-Mommy hearts, you are unwilling to douse their hopeless but genuine enthusiasm, you consent.

So your tour of the place begins. And a more glistening, luxurious gym you have never seen. I mean, remember that first gym back in Alhambra in 1970? It was one of Jack La Lanne's first, and it was a dingy, odiferous, bare basics, hard working, no-frills affair? Remember that? You adored it. You were twenty-one and it was there you would suffer your first major injury in the pursuit of body perfect.

This current day gym is not that, and if you weren't so intent on getting to the chlorine-free pool, the sheer amount of gleaming steel and serenity inspired, eucalyptus infused locker rooms, yoga rooms, dance rooms, Pilates studios, saunas, steam rooms, the big glistening machines themselves in the center of the place, the basket ball court outside, where, glimmering just beyond is that pool, to finally the discrete amount of customers actually working out in the place, this palatial ode to physical fitness would fill you with such an admiration and indeed awe, you would be ready to consent to anything other than swimming in the swimming pool.

So, you do ooh and aah for the next half hour. You are polite, indeed enthusiastic. But when you finally crack, it's when they're showing you the juice bar. It is a juice bar that is fit for a king, but you really really don't care.

You turn to their fresh and dewy faces and firmly state, "I'm here because I want one thing and one thing only. I want to swim here. So show me the salt water pool," you say, your own eyes now steely and unforgiving.

Their bright, happy eyes dim. You will never get the body you want just swimming in that stupid pool, their big eyes say.

But finally *finally* I'm led to the shimmering pool, the one in which I know, I just know, my ailing back will find relief. And there it lies. All turquoise poise and thick white towels. It beckons me. It loves me.

I still shun bathing suit activities if I don't feel glamorous enough to don a bathing suit. I still say why. I still derive pleasure from feeling self-assured enough to admit it.

But I do have a bathing suit. I have two, even though the saltwater swimming pool at the gym and I have parted ways. I found that Speedo and other straight-forward athletic swimming suits give a certain je ne sais quoi to even the most rattled body. They have this Parisian minimalism. They are the LBD of bathing suits. They are downtown.

So that sometimes, with my dashing Speedo and my emerging I'm a goddess attitude, I can be enticed to put on a bathing suit. And sometimes, like last summer, this meant I put on the Speedo because I didn't want to miss the opportunity to jump off a yacht in the sapphire blue Aegean Ocean to swim like a porpoise, the beautiful Greek Islands my backdrop.

The Purse

The Purse.
Without which we cannot live.
Coach. Prada. Gucci. Chanel. Vintage. The Handmade Street Fair. Your Daughter's Reject. Your Husband's Briefcase. Your back pocket—
Okay, no. Not the back pocket. Except for the few fully grown tomboys who believe they are above the law of iPhones being texted accidentally while seated...

Why do women carry purses and men don't? Because men have pockets in their pants and jackets, and we don't? Because they aren't as vain as we are and don't need to carry their hair gel with them? Because they have freedom and we don't?

I mean what on earth is our excuse for the trunks we carry around with us?

Not even when they have the kids with them, do men feel the need to carry a purse. There are no single fathers suddenly carrying purses around, even though they are on kid duty, picking them up from school and doing the grocery store shopping.

Men are able to leave the house with the keys, their wallet

and cell phone, and call it a day. Even if they've reached the age of reading glasses those are stashed in their inside jacket pockets. Even if they have the tickets, there are more inside pockets for those.

Why can't a woman be more like a man?

But more to the point, why is my purse so heavy?

I was sixteen when I began to need a purse. I turned sixteen, got a driver's license, and had to carry that license with me in order to drive the car. So in order to carry the shiny new license safely, I had to put it into a shiny new wallet, which, at first I did put in my pocket. The wallet, however, soon needed money in it as well, obviously, for things like gas and those In-n-Out Burgers one had to lie to Mom about having eaten just before dinner—

Soon the wallet weighed more than it should have.

And this was before my wallet also began carrying credit cards, car insurance cards, health insurance cards, ATM cards, Costco cards, grocery store cards, AAA cards, Bloomingdale cards, Alaska Airlines cards—

You don't carry an Alaska Airlines card?

So the wallet had to be carried in a purse because my hip pocket wasn't a cool location for it at all. Not at all…and besides, somehow, yes, by now, I wanted a purse.

My mother, a lover of all things purse, had been offering them to me for years. Especially the luminous beaded bags she'd gotten in Belgium, a country known for its beautiful beading. I did have those. But I needed a day bag. A purse. A luscious soft leather, or happy straw, or decadent beaded, or hippy fringed. I didn't know exactly. I didn't care. All I knew was I now needed a purse in which to carry my wallet.

That was the start—
Of life with The Purse.

These days my purse is always a handsome devil. Expensive and chic. But I only have one purse and I use it everyday. Once in a great while I'll grudgingly carry an evening bag which barely helps me survive the evening out. But then it's right back to the same old friend. Because these days…and for a long time…it hasn't been about the purse. It is about what I put in it.

I'm not sure when I began to add and add and add to my purse. I'm vague as to when it began that I needed so much stuff every time I stepped out the door I should have had an assistant to help. But it happened.

It must have been gradual, this life exercise of piling its onerous issues upon my sloping shoulders. First that driver's license. Then the stuff needed to survive the date with the boyfriend. Then the stuff needed to go to work with me. At some point a husband was added, and yes, I carried his wallet and other accoutrement in my purse as well.

I added and added…until I hit that apex of purse necessities, the absolute pinnacle of leaving the house weighed down by everything I simply must have…just in case—

I am referring, of course, to the days of child-raising. More specifically when this involved babies and needing to carry diapers, handiwipes, Desitin, pacifiers, stuffed animals, sippy cups, snacks, a change of clothing for the baby, a change of clothing for the toddler, a change of clothing for me, as well as several other items I have happily obliterated from my mind, because those were dark days indeed.

However, I'm finding it continues. It gets worse and worse.

And now my shoulders are shouting "I'm not going to take it anymore."

I am sure my purse is more loaded down these days than when I was at the height of child-raising, when I needed everything in the house to accompany me when I ventured out with my precious and fragile cargo...I mean children.

Here I am now, minus children, minus husband, and my purse is heavier than ever. And okay, I'll say it. My shoulders are tired. They hurt. They are beginning to fall apart. Particularly the right one. You guessed it. My purse carrying shoulder.

But my purse doesn't care. It just opens its greedy mouth and demands more and more and more—

Is this part of the aging psyche I haven't thought of yet? Do I need more *because* I'm getting older? Do I need more to feel safe in a world that is ever so slowly starting to move faster than I am?

If so, I need a personal assistant. An issue I will begin working on. Maybe a live-in housekeeper...a driver too...

But I digress...

Purses.

My purse, to be exact...although maybe you'll see yours here too.

My purse now holds four pairs of glasses—my reading glasses, my regular glasses, and two pairs of sunglasses—one prescription and one non-prescription...I won't even go into the gargantuan size and weight of their cases. Actually I've taken steps there in that I've ditched the obnoxious cases for weightless jewelry bags in which the glasses appear to be surviving.

I have a flashlight for reading the menu. I'm particularly proud of that bit of foresight. However, I got it before I realized my phone too has a flashlight. So I could ditch the flashlight, but I don't want to. It's such a gorgeous shade of metallic aqua, is slender, indeed sylph-like, and has that sexy je ne sais quoi when produced in a darkened restaurant on that sexy date. It lessens the dramatic statement of where I am in my life's journey the reading glasses may or may not impart, also given my dining companion is usually very happy to see if the flashlight works on his menu too.

There's the all-important cell phone. The modern miracle that I adore and never turn off and do everything obnoxious you can do with it...except have loud conversations in public. No. Instead I text...and text and text and text... My children will attest to that, my friends, my finance guy, the Pilates studio, my sister-in-laws...my brothers, for that matter...

There are the combs, the eye drops (thank heavens for eye drops, right?), the Band-Aids...you carry Band-Aids too, don't you?

There's Kleenex. These little packets totally come in handy. They keep making them cuter too. I was introduced to them by my second husband. I thought he was being incredibly prissy. Until I discovered their charms. Now I feel an alarm akin to leaving my cell phone at home when I run out of them. It's so bad I've even bought them at airports, running to catch a plane.

The keys, oh those keys. Heavier than a monk's mammoth bronze key ring, and that man is carrying every key there is in the monastery.

When did my keys get so heavy? It's not like I have six houses, four cars, or even one gate to get into.

At first I thought it was the key chain making all the weight. I had an especially wonderful one from Paris bought at La Monnaie. And attached to that I still had the one that says "Mom", now fading, which my daughter bought me when she was six years old. One does not need to use two key chains to carry one set of keys. So reluctantly I've removed the heavy Parisian one. I love Paris, but I adore my daughter. And every time I see that key ring saying 'Mom', I remember exactly what she looked like at six.

But now I seem to have extra keys on it in spite of myself. This is even after divesting the key chain of the keys that went with my old house. This is even after removing all the duplicate keys. This is after eliminating the keys to my ex-husband's car. He hasn't had that car in years. And this is even after tossing out those two tiny mystery keys I've carried around, just in case, for thirty years. The thing still weighs a ton.

I also carry a camera. It's as small as I can get and still have the oomph to take an actual picture. But it's a clunker in my purse. Especially as I keep it in its case. The case is described as lightweight, and I suppose it is. But somehow, even that ounce or two makes a difference.

Then there is the makeup case. Given I don't wear that much, I continue to be amazed about what I must absolutely have with me. The most important being lipstick and a mirror with which to refresh it.

Speaking of the joys of refreshing my lipstick in public? I know there are rules about how, where and when. Something like one can refresh their lipstick right there at the restaurant table at lunch. But by dinner this is a social gaffe so big one can never recover even a lingering shred of dignity should one choose to defy convention.

I have done so anyway. And I swear to you, I still have a shred of dignity.

There are always the extras, the occaisionals, the may-bes, the last minute toss-ins and purchases.

In Europe and Florida I carry an umbrella in my purse.

Usually I'm wearing my scarf, but sometimes I carry it in my purse, like in case I'm going to see a movie on a hot day and need armor against the theater's air-conditioning.

Sometimes there's a baseball hat. Sometimes there's an iPad. The last I'm trying not to encourage.

Sometimes there's a bag of donuts. I refuse to explain on the grounds this may incriminate me.

There might be a playbill or two, a tweezers, several pens, a small notebook, maybe a map, even though I have the all-knowing phone. Sometimes a pair of gloves and an extra tote…this usually in Paris where they don't believe in providing you with bags for your purchases—

And other stuff.

But so, this is why my purse is so heavy? In spite of the fact I no longer need to carry my children or husbands with me?

Why?

Can I whittle it down? Apply scientific logic and gut instinct to sum this situation up?

I have come to the conclusion it is because we women are a cozy breed. We like things comfortable. We like to make the people around us comfortable. We're nice that way.

In a pinch we can whip something out of our purses that will save the day. This happens over and over. I've done it. You've done it. I've seen it being done.

That bandaid, those extra drugstore reading glasses, that piece of butterscotch, that scrap of paper and pen, that extra binky…for the dog.

When our man or our children or our friends or even the

family behind us in the movie theater sees one of us beautiful women swing into action to begin rummaging through our purses, an instant sense of relief washes over them. Because they know better than us it's going to be all right. Because they know better than us that not only can we save the day with what we have in our purses, we could probably save the world. And they know this will never change. Because within that purse is the personification of what is within each of us. The desire and ability to nurture.

So that we carry our purses, stuffed full of glorious, everyday things to keep our comfy selves feeling comfy and whole and able, even out in the big, wide world.

Currently my purse is an olive green Coach. I bought it on-line from a warehouse sale. It will last me a year. I have been lightening its load as best I can. I no longer carry that extra flashlight, for instance. No old playbills either.

Today someone picked it up and exclaimed, "Wow! This is the lightest purse I have ever held!"

I felt instant panic. I quickly ran through the contents.

Bandaids—check.

Last week's seat assignment flying home from Oregon—check.

Scarf because I was going to the movies—check.

Amber oil—check.

Swiss knife—check.

Whew. All was well.

I was okay, and would still be able to save the world should the need arise.

꙳

Cleaning Lady

A butcher, a baker, a candlestick maker. A daughter, a wife, a niece, and an aunt. A landlady, a leasee, a mommy and stepmommy. A writer, a runner, a yogi, and eater. A part time vegetarian, a fulltime crossword solver, I run up the mountain and slide back down. I call a job many things, and I call many things a job.

And then one year this job came along.

"It's easy money."

We were standing by the opened trunk of her car looking down at a vacuum cleaner. She wasn't the sort of girl to have a vacuum cleaner. She was a trainer at my gym in Laguna Beach. Blond and thin and young. She should have had marijuana plants or a snowboard or extra bikinis in her trunk. Not this vacuum cleaner, lying on its side looking like the most pointless item in the world.

I was newly divorced. Newly back in Southern California after the divorce. Newly single mother with two small children. Newly back home close to Mom and Dad—

Living the good life in Laguna Beach.

I was developing a cartoon strip about single parenting. The easel for my drawings was in my bedroom, but I was able to separate work and sleep easily.

I worked out at the gym, I took ballet at Ballet Pacifica, and I ran four miles a day. I loved my rented house. I loved my children's school. I loved loved loved everything about my life, except…except I was running though my money like Christmas was tomorrow, and I had told my gym friend this.

We were standing by her car after a particularly good work out, and she re-iterated, "Easy money and as much as you want. They're desperate in Laguna. I couldn't believe how desperate!"

I eyed the vacuum cleaner distrustfully. "I don't want to have to drag my stuff over."

"Don't worry, they have all the stuff. This is mine. I just got it repaired."

"How much did you say they pay?" She said it again. "A few houses a week, and you are talking some nice cash."

"I can barely keep my own clean, " I said. "It's hard work."

"Not when you're getting paid to do it."

We were talking house cleaning. Other peoples' houses. We were talking cleaning ladies. The cleaning ladies being her and me. She was already doing it.

The lazy good-for-nothing in me rose up. I hated cleaning my own house.

Besides, I just knew the homeowners would look at me funny. They'd be suspicious. I didn't emanate hardworking, scrubbing vibes. I emanated an I-don't-care-about-your-house vibes.

"No way they'll even notice you," said my friend. "They won't even look at you. They don't care anything about you, just that you come in and in four hours change their pigsty into something halfway decent."

I was wavering. This idea was certainly more feasible than the call girl idea my friend had suggested last month. Although, heck yeah, I'd considered it. I gave it a glamorous spin when I told my sisters about it. I started working on my tan. Then my youngest sister called me up. "Drop it," she said. "Drop the call girl thing. It's so wrong. You have two little kids." When I still tried to bluff my way into going for it, she snarled, "I'll tell Mom and Dad." I blanched. And Ruth Yunker, Call Girl, never made it onto my resumé. Mom and Dad were able to continue loving me in good faith.

But so, I still needed extra money. And my gym pal had come up with this. "I've been doing it for two years. It's not bad. There's always work. You can go straight from the gym in your workout clothes. It's cash. And it's only for four hours."

"What if I don't finish in four hours?"

"You *can* finish in four hours. Kitchen, bathrooms, vacuum, maybe a little dusting if you have time, which normally depends on the number of bathrooms—"

"But even so—"

"You leave after four hours, no matter what. They shouldn't leave things so messy in the first place."

And so it came to be that one day right after my ballet class I was standing in the doll-like home of the owner of the gym where I worked out. "It's all pretty straightforward," she said. "But are you sure you're up for it?" She looked at me appraisingly. "You don't strike me as the cleaning lady sort. What happened to the cartoon strip idea?"

"Still working on it," I said. She nodded. This was Laguna Beach, a town rife with struggling artists.

She turned out to live in one of the most fairytale houses

in Laguna Beach. It was a mini English Tudor cottage. I adored this house. I regularly drove by it just to have a look. During the twenties Hollywood stars came down to Laguna for the ocean and built these mini Hansel and Gretel vacation cottages. This was one of the few left standing, and it was obviously her pride and joy. I was supposed to clean her pride and joy?

She took me around, showing me what she needed done, and told me how she liked it done. Here were all the implements of torture—vacuum, cleaning fluids, rags. I'd been told to bring my own rubber gloves. After the pep talk, and assuring me that she was an easy woman to work for, she departed, leaving me to clean her precious house. For money. She left the money in an envelope on the top of the desk in the fairytale living room.

Only then did the reality of the situation make itself felt. I was standing in a house in which, over the next four hours, I was going to scrub, vacuum, wipe, dust, room after room after toilet bowl. It was going to be hard work. It was going to be grimy work. It was going to be precise work—she had these little diamond paned windows in the kitchen and dining room, for instance, which she wanted done. They weren't windows per se, so I hadn't refused or anything stupid like that. But my heart had sunk. Windows and mirrors are bears for precision neatniks like myself. Hence my angst cleaning my own house. Perfection always turned the job into a nightmare.

So, performance anxiety hovered. Along with sheer loathing for the work.

It was late morning. It was a beautiful clear day in Laguna Beach. The scent of the air was ocean breeze and jasmine. I wanted to go home. I wanted my mother. I wanted my children. I wanted a way out—

Slowly, I headed for the kitchen. In my own house I always started with the kitchen. I'd do the same here. Man up, I said to self. There's a jug of pistachio ice cream in it for you when it's all over.

And some money.

I lasted six months.

After six months I looked up one day and decided I wanted to raise my children back on the East Coast after all. I decided that the life I was leading in Laguna Beach was the life of a teenager or twenty year old, and I needed the discipline of the East Coast. I decided my kids needed East Coast schools. I decided that it was foolish to still own a nice big house in Baltimore rented out to strangers while I crawled around in Laguna Beach cleaning other people's houses, and not exactly shining at it.

The straw that broke the camel's back was the house in which I had already ruined the woman's entry floor, so frankly, I don't know why she kept adding to my duties. On paper these additional chores weren't so bad—like watering her outdoor potted plants. Except, like with everything else in her house, there were a lot of them, they were fussy plants, and watering them added to the time it was already taking me to get everything else done.

One day she left a note asking me to clean out her outdoor cats' litter box which was in the crawl space under her front porch. I crouched down to have a look. It was a no man's land of kitty feces under there. It reeked of cat urine.

And at that moment my own house back in Maryland, setting on an acre in a forest, danced up in front of me, and I was suddenly struck with the necessity of moving back to Baltimore.

Over the six months I had accumulated six houses. I turned down at least that many more. My friend had been right about the quantity. However, six was more than enough.

One was that fairytale house. My first house. It was so pretty. The gym owner was so precise that I'm sure I never got it quite to her standards, but she never complained. She was an entrepreneur in that arty little town, and open to helping those less fortunate than herself.

Then came the regular suburban house up in Arch Heights. This was a family of four children and two parents who worked. This was a house that had four bedrooms and I don't know how many bathrooms, because I only ever made it to one. Because this was a house in which the parents had long ago lost control of the situation and given up.

I would arrive to a kitchen piled high with dirty dishes, pans still on the stove, a disposal that only worked intermittently, books, clothes and dog dishes scattered all over. It was a nightmare kitchen. The only thing that saved it was it had good bones. It was dying to be a nice kitchen. Even a pretty kitchen. It was light and bright. It was big. It would have even been roomy if you could actually see it. But it also took me almost two hours to pull it together. The stove alone required a masters' degree in cleaning.

So this didn't leave me much time for all the rest. I left the mother a note after the first go-round saying as much, and she replied to skip the kids' bedrooms (thank you!) and to please focus on the master bathroom, the floors, the kitchen and vacuuming. Her vacuum cleaner had an excessively short cord. I have no patience with vacuum cleaners and their cords.

In one room, so filled with furniture the vacuum cleaner's short cord made it only possible to vacuum the very center of the room, that I eventually made the executive decision that the center of the room was enough. If this was how badly the family was going to treat their house, well, I would only do what I could and resist calling in the cavalry to finish the job.

When I resigned, I resigned by leaving them a note on the kitchen table. I was polite, so I lied. Instead of saying "Your house is a pigsty. You're lucky you don't have roaches. You need to throw out half your furniture and all the kids, and you need a longer cord on that pathetic vacuum cleaner of yours," I wrote, "Thank you for the opportunity to work for you, but I can't clean your house anymore because I'm moving back East." She responded by calling up and begging me to stay. She offered to double my fee. There was panic in her voice. But I was running as fast as I could. Her desperation was no match for mine.

The cat lady with the litter box underneath the porch was a business woman whose overbearing manner and appearance belied the delicacy of her home's décor. It was filled with glass, porcelain, mirrored surfaces, silk drapes that dragged on the floor, glass tiles that required a certain cleanser to retain their sheen. Every surface, which were glass or marble or custom made tile, was covered with delicate, antique, expensive and breakable baubles. They were all things of beauty. The whole place was like a window of Tiffany's at Christmas—a wonderland of gorgeousness around which you could not move for fear of smashing something. You definitely could not sit down. Even her bed had such an intricate array of pillows and placing, that she ultimately left me a diagram of where each pillow was to be placed, and how it was to be plumped...a concept I hadn't heard of until then.

Hers was the place where I'd ruined the front entry floor. She had some sort of glassy, marble-like tile on the floor.

Quite beautiful, of course. I'm sure it glowed in the dark. In fact her whole place had a kind of aquatic underwater beauty. I figured she was a Pisces.

I was uncertain how to clean the entry floor, even though it looked (and probably was) already clean. Today I would probably just rub it down with water and a soft cloth, followed by a kind of buffing dry with another soft cloth. But then I thought I needed to use a cleanser from a bottle on it, if for no other reason than to show I had "cleaned" it.

I forget what I used. But it was a disaster. It left a milky film on it, which never went away, no matter how many other products I tried on it. Including what my mother suggested when I called her desperately one day. The woman wasn't happy. When I finally said I didn't know how to fix her floor, that maybe she should get professional floor people in here to look at it, she said, looking me squarely in the face. "I thought you were the professional here." I stared back, standing there in my yoga clothes.

My note to her said nothing about the disgusting cat boxes underneath the house. Nor did it apologize for the entry floor. I figured they balanced each other out. Her note said, "I've decided to move back East, so I won't be coming back."

She did not call me up begging.

One of the houses had a skylight in the kitchen and Cool Whip in the freezer. I remember nothing other about the place except that where the California sun glared down through the skylight in the middle of the kitchen was a place to be avoided for fear of being burnt to death. It's here I learned that skylights have hidden dangers people don't think of, and I'm not talking about leaking when it rains.

The other was that Cool Whip. I couldn't leave it alone. I kept coming back to it, dipping tiny little spoonfuls out through out the entire four hours I was there. They never seemed to run out of this Cool Whip. And I was never able to leave it alone.

In fact snacking was also an issue at the fairy tale cottage of the gym owner. She always had cashews. I couldn't leave those alone either. And she never ran out of them just like the Cool Whip people never ran out of Cool Whip.

They couldn't have been on to me, could they?

I've been a candlestick maker, a wife and a writer. I've been a mother-in-law, a single mother and an eater of grape popsicles.

I've been a cleaning woman too.

I didn't like the work. Which helped alert me to the fact I wasn't on the straight path headed where I hoped to go. It alerted me that my path had veered off backwards. So I gave up the free Cool Whip and cashews.

I packed up my six year old son and four year old daughter and moved back East. And the path suddenly straightened, new doors opened up, and I was back on track.

Now, I'm in the latter stage of my life. Society encourages staying put and nestling safely into what one knows for "people my age". Especially if things are going well.

But when what I'm doing is getting on my nerves, I know this is a signal to me to look up-

And seriously consider the hot new idea.

Because maybe the list of what I've been isn't finished.

Old Ladies Settin
'Round 'n Talkin'

They are a part of the fabric at every wedding, every funeral, every family reunion, every river front barbecue, every Thanksgiving Day celebration. You know who they are.

They are those fabulous old gals over there, havin' all that fun, settin' round 'n talkin'. They are your aunts or great aunts. They are your cousins once removed. They are the grandmother of Joey and Susan and Samuel. They are Al and Tom and Julianna's great aunt.

Maybe their husbands are still alive. Maybe not. But no men are in evidence. Their self-contained enjoyment of each others' company brooks no male interference unless the male is a son, a nephew or grandson, or any boy under the age of twenty who wants to come over for a quick little flirt. And they do, those boys, they do want to come over for a little flirt because nobody knows how to flirt better than these fabulous gals.

There they are in shaded corners in the park. They are always a colorful group. A haphazard array of floral, light-weight, and easy-going clothing. Bought from wherever was closest the day they needed something. Maybe even a garage sale.

They are usually wearing hats to keep the sun off, even under that tree. In the old days these were real hats, big and floppy. Now they can just as easily be visors, also big, but not floppy.

The fabulous old gals fan as they talk. With napkins, hats, actual fans. I think it's built in as women age, this fanning business, and it started with menopause, or the result of having grown up in the South...as was the case with my mother and aunties.

Their chairs don't match. Lawn chairs, fold out chairs, beach chairs, even when a beach is nowhere in sight, are scattered in a lopsided circle. There are blankets, but no one is about to creek their bones all the way down to the hard grass, blanket or no blanket. If they run out of chairs, they look up and wave at the closest male. He knows immediately what they need, and hustles off to find a chair. Heck, make that two or three chairs, even if it means the younger generation lose theirs.

They sit in that comfy circle. They laugh a lot, throwing themselves onto the back of their chairs. They lean in towards each other as they gossip with abandon. They drink, thoroughly. They eat with abandon, especially when the cake shows up. They kick off their tennis shoes and sandals and flipflops. Their purses are near enough to be in their sight, but otherwise, they are just satchels to be picked up at the end of the day. Cell phones are nowhere to be seen.

They are universal, this group. And we love them.

Especially...because we are not them...yet.

My Aunt Marcella, visiting from Mom's hometown Louisville, was settin' 'round the backyard yackin' with my mother and some of her friends. They were drinking ice tea. The kind that in Louisville sits on the back burner of the stove in a chili-making pot, brewing all day. I came out to say 'hey'. (My Southern accent comes on whenever any of my Louisville aunties are nearby). It was getting long about four-thirty. I asked my blond Aunt Marcella if she'd like some more ice tea. She laughed. "Oh honey, no. It's time for bourbon. (No one can drawl the word bourbon like a Louisville native). I asked how she'd like it. She held out her ice tea glass, the one that still had ice tea in it, and said "Pour it right in here, darlin'." I went into the house, got the bourbon, and came out to pour a good slosh of booze into each proffered ice tea glass. No fussin' over pointless details like ice or not. Then they all went back to settin' 'round 'n talkin'.

So then there's us. Okay, me. But may I use 'us' here, so that I don't feel alone, so very very alone, in this cruel rite of passage?

We're the middle-aged women who are taut, chic, pulled together, handling it all, including the aging thing. We're totally cool, if we do say so ourselves. We hang with the likes of Cyndi Lauper and Susan Sarandon, and if we're really feeling confident, Charlotte Rampling. We're doing this with the help of Botox, therapy, huge amounts of exercise, and that wavering but still very brave ego we never used to think twice about.

When we see these intrepid women settin' 'round and having fun just yammerin', we see our future and are afraid. Because we don't want what they have, see. Not now, not ever. Got it?

But there they sit, happy as kittens, relaxed as saints. Something middle-aged women like me haven't been since we gave birth.

But then, one day something happens. Something organic. In spite of ourselves, we begin to, ever so vaguely, understand these women.

This settling in, this letting go, this just not caring anymore, so unpleasant to us now, so frightening to us now, begins to raise it's head. Just here and there. Only once in awhile—

Nature easing us in.

We may gradually become aware that quite unobtrusively we've stopped caring about some minor issue about which we use to be passionate. This happens so quietly we don't even notice. And if we do notice, we put it down to feeling more relaxed now because the children are finally out of college, the puppy is an old lady and doesn't need a walk three times a day, and the five mile run feels redundant. Instead that elegant Pilates studio just down the street, with classes that start at 10:00 instead of 6:30 am, and has instructors our age, is the place to be.

We're all different in just where these easy-going adjustments might show up. But we are not different in the way they work. The Thing, the thing we thought would never ever change? We suddenly notice it isn't in the picture anymore. And it feels organic.

I lived on the beach for ten years, and it was during this time that I gave up the romantic stroll on the beach after dinner. Because I realized, slowly but surely, the romantic stroll along the beach was in reality a big fat pain in the... well never mind.

It was organic, actually, the realization that I was totally over the romantic walk on the beach. The wind, the sand, the sun in my eyes—

Over the walk on the beach?

Wait a minute! I heard a bell! The warning bell that said I was on some kind of slippery slope. I couldn't, I wouldn't, say the words aloud, but they were there. The slippery slope to complacent old age.

No way.

I paused. I contemplated my quitting the walk on the beach. What had happened to it being right up there with flying business on an overseas flight?

Okay, it was a pain in the neck to even get out the door to walk on that romantic beach.

There, I said it.

It was like…should I or should I not wear shoes while taking this stroll? If it was winter, yes. But of course I'd bring a mother lode of sand back into the house when I got back, no matter how careful I was, no matter how anal… including removing the shoes before I was within spitting distance of the door. If it were summer, well, okay I'd go out with bare feet, those nice clean feet I had just scrubbed up from the afternoon on the beach.

Did I need sunscreen? I hate sunscreen. The stuff burns my skin. Well maybe the sun was low enough in the sky already. Which meant it would glare into my eyes for at least one direction of the walk…

Should I wear a hat? But that would ruin my hair. But the wind was blowing. Of course. The wind was always blowing on the beach, and it was always enough to ruin my hair.

Should I wear sunglasses?

The actual walking on sand was a pain in the neck. Each step slipped in the sand just enough to make it hard work, this soulful stroll on the beach. Just enough to threaten sciatica. Just enough to work up a sweat in spite of the wind.

We could walk down by the water where the sand was

wet, therefore hard. But there one walked on a slant at this beach where I lived. Walking at a slant tilted my already unstable pelvis even more out of whack. Just enough to potentially double that dose of sciatica.

Either one direction or the other, the setting sun glared straight into my eyes.

Finally, the wind blew in my face in one direction or the other. Particularly awful were those strolls on the beach during which the sun *and* the wind were assaulting my face at the same time.

Instead, if I simply chose to stay in after dinner, allowing my meal to digest peacefully, there would be wonderful times settin' on the deck. I could gaze peacefully out at the big blue ocean, listen to the glorious waves, smell the delicious sea air, all without working up a sweat, a stitch in my side, and ruining my hair.

This became blindingly clear to me one summer evening as I managed to escape the stroll and waved goodbye to the others as they straggled out the door. They were already clutching at their hats. They were already walking at a slant into the wind, across the quick-sand beach. They were already looking cold and tired. Probably regretting having eaten so much at dinner. I saw all that as I sat on the deck on a comfortable chair, eating a piece of cake, chatting with my mother, and feeling complete contentment.

So happily, right then and there, I stopped walking on the beach after dinner.

Oh, I pretended chagrin on forgoing the walk, but I waved happily as everyone else left for the post dinner stroll. I skipped around the house the minute they trudged off, looking like a sad group setting off for a trek in the Himalayas.

Now I stand here, watching my particular batch of elderly relatives. And I am aware they are looking less and less alien.

This process eased into my awareness slowly, cautiously.

Ever aware, however subliminally, I was on a slippery slope to acceptance…of old age, at first I began to recognize what my elder women used to look like, particularly when they were my age. And I saw they had been beautiful in so many ways.

So it was at this point old age started to feel less alien. It was still un-acceptable. Don't get me wrong. Certainly not in the kind of old age that consisted of being too content to not care what the younger generation thought. But old age had certainly begun to look real. These vivacious elderly women start to look real. I found this comforted me. Becoming like them was still frightening, but at the same time, more recognizable. More feasible.

Then the day came. I looked at them and not only recognize they had been beautiful once, I looked at them and saw that they were beautiful *now*. They were vivacious, joyful, involved beauties right now, canes and hearing aids and a certain querulous attitude not withstanding.

Which meant, and here fear threatened to sweep back in, I was so close to becoming an old woman, the edge of the cliff appeared at my feet, and I was inches away from the moment I would trip and stumble down to the hideous, inevitable fall into old age, as if I had never been young, and for certain never would be again.

Except-

Along the way, just before the fall off the ledge into old age, I had seen that there was nothing to fear, because when

the moment happens, I will have already eased into it. In fact, I won't have noticed, much like those long gone and never missed trudges on the windswept beach.

Staring at my comfy old women, my beautiful old aunties and second cousins and all, a warm, fuzzy feeling is suddenly able to rise up within my still chic, but progressively more battered body because—

Those old ladies? Those talky old biddies? Those mothers, editors, lawyers, homemakers, sales persons, advertising execs, photographers, school principals, professors, entrepreneurs...

They're starting to look not so bad. In fact, they're starting to look mighty darn fine. Sitting around like that. Having fun.

They are a bunch of amazing beauties who have beat the odds.

They are a bunch of wise crones who have all the magic they need because they have done it all.

And they are happy. I can see it with my own eyes. They are happy, proud, and undiminished. And they know it.

"Hey kid, come over here. Get me some cake, sonny. And bring me a chair. Place it just on the outside of the circle, but near enough so I can hear." Because I'm still learning how I'm going to do this.

And everyone of them pretends they don't see me—
Except just out of the corner of their eagle eyes.

Tiny Elderly Woman and the Elevator

The elevator door was too heavy for a heavy weight boxer, let alone the elderly, Chihuahua-sized dynamo, even now yanking it open and holding it wide for me. I had one purse sliding off my shoulder, one plastic bag containing one roll of toilet paper, a box of saran wrap, Bordeaux cookies, and a desperate look on my face. I could see it reflected in the rusted grate of the elevator. Or maybe I just intuited it, because the elderly woman had sprung into action the minute the rattling elevator had arrived.

The elevator arrived, and I knew, I just knew, although I was feeling particularly elderly myself that day, I just knew that I was the one who should be leaping forward to deal with the elevator. Not the miniscule elderly woman standing there, even now, apparently without effort, holding the door open for me.

This elevator was a relic from, well, I don't know when. I'd seen the like in old movies. And even the movie *The King's Speech* in which one of these elevators was featured. I'd laughed along with the rest of the audience when upon finding themselves in an elevator waiting for it to move upward, the king and queen of England suddenly realized they had to do something all by themselves in order to alert the machine as to their needs.

I came to New York, staying for six weeks in a charming apartment in a wonderful pre-war building–I don't know which war. I used to be very good at history, but I no longer have confidence. I want to say pre-WWI, but who knows. Vietnam wasn't in my history books growing up, but ever since the day I saw it in *my* children's history books, I realized me and my kind were already being relegated to the attic of historical times. This realization was further cemented when I heard my very own sixties era referred to as *mid-century*. I'm now afraid to commit…to so many things in general. But specifically to which war pre-war buildings refer to in the frightening world of NYC real estate.

The elevator, in this vaguely hostile pre-war building, was not the kind which did all the work. In fact the first time it came down, I stood there for three hours waiting for it to make a move. Like slide open or something, indicating to me, the polite newcomer, that it was willing to allow me in, and indeed carry me to any floor I might want. I was, to be precise, willing and able to push a floor button. As far as I knew one is still required to do that. That elevators, even the most advanced, still need to be told which floor. They are not yet mind readers. Although, come to think of it, why we couldn't just call out the number of the floor we want. Wouldn't that be nice? Or would various accents get in the way. For instance, Texan accents would not be understood by any Yankee elevators. Or the Parisian elevators simply being unwilling to deal with any accent at all, except of the born and bred Parisian from the 7th arrondissement.

But so, that day, early in my stay in NYC, I suddenly realized I would have to open the door myself if I expected anything else to happen.

I pulled it open. That is, after two tries, I got the heavy-weight door open. But that wasn't good enough. The door now open, next there was this grate/gate contraption. I'd definitely seen these in old movies. Very old movies. The grate came next. It required to be slid sideways. I couldn't do it.

But here the situation was. The heavy as an elephant door needed to by held open while pulling open the equally immovable grate. I didn't have the muscle power to do it. I do yoga. I don't lift weights. I panicked. I would have to climb six flights of stairs one million times during the six weeks I was going to be here in this bleak pre-war apartment building because the elevator wouldn't stand aside and let me in.

Get a grip—

What a phrase, right? But clean and neat too, so that it can slide in and take charge when the rest of the modern brain is still waiting for the miracle to happen. Like waiting for the elevator to open easily, noiselessly, efficiently, all by itself.

Get. A. Grip.

Manpower strode in. My body remembered the time I lifted weights. Not heavy, of course, but enough that the visual of a body builder swept in. And of course if that didn't work, I could call on memories of all the times I found myself carrying a storming three year old out of wherever.

Heave ho! I hauled the heavy outer door open wide enough so that I could slide my body between it and the grate. Success!

Now I channeled a massive tree trunk withstanding hurricane winds. I took a deep breath, and with both hands, feet panted firmly on the ground, I hauled the grate open. I stepped in.

Stepping in was a mistake. I should have leapt in. I should have leapt in like I had a rabid dog on my tail.

Instead I stepped in, releasing both grate and my position holding open the heavy outer door. The grate banged shut. Who knew the thing could move that fast. I mean, I could hardly drag it open. But snap shut it did, leaving my hand and part of my shoulder on the wrong side. And then the outer door crashed onto the rest of my shoulder. I think part of my foot was still out there too.

I stared at the corner of the wall I was facing, trapped. Trapped like the useless tourist I was. Trapped like the climbers on Mt Everest when Mother Nature has taken offence. Trapped on the ground floor of a pre-war building, who knew which war—

Merely by trying to get up to the sixth floor where my apartment was even now wondering where the heck I was. My heart beat wildly—

Get. A. Grip.

Did its magic again. Now I, with the strength of Goliath, heaved first the grate, then the door, open. I leapt to freedom.

I was now back out in the hall, breathing heavily. The two doors to the elevator had banged shut with such force, I expected the fire department to send a rescue crew. Banged with such force that yes, I took it personally.

Well, I wasn't going to take this lying down. I was a grown woman. I knew my way around, okay? I rode the metros in Paris. I rode the subways right here in NYC. I drove the LA freeways at rush hour and still got where I was going on time, okay? I could do this elevator. This smirking, belligerent, this truly imbecilic elevator. I could take it any day.

I started again. Prepared this time. Using every muscle I never knew I had, I hauled open the outer door. I wedged myself in between it and the grate. I took a moment to adjust my purse to the front of my body, like it was my new name tag. Then I, roaring silently…I hope silently…dragged the ugly, ancient, useless grate open. Now both doors were open. But I wouldn't be able to sustain the weight of both doors for long, determined as they were to slam shut like the wrath of Zeus. I checked my position. Good. All was in order. I could do this! I took another breath, and I leapt inside the elevator, letting go of each door as I did. There was a mind-boggling crash as each slammed shut behind me. I paused a moment, expecting to find I'd miscalculated and lost a hand in the process. But no. No pain. No. It seemed all of me was in.

Inner sirens went off! The triumph! The awe-inspiring triumph! I was in the elevator, in one piece. I could have floated up to the sixth floor at this point—

Maybe that's why it took a moment to realize I had one more task to get the thing moving. Oh yeah. Okay. Right. I knew that! I pushed button six.

And with a lurch, the old contraption began to move upward.

"Thank you," I said now, to my elderly benefactor. "I think these doors are going to do me in," I said.

She laughed. "Mind over matter, my dear," she said. "Works on everything, I find. Including these cold-blooded doors. I lost a dog to them once."

I blanched.

"Just a little joke, my dear. To brighten your New York day."

Eating with Our Hands

When I ask myself what it means to be an American woman, the answer arrives as smooth as a duck landing on choppy water. What it means to be an American woman is to savor eating food that runs down her arms. The true American woman neither shies away from such food because it is messy, nor because it's fattening. She embraces such food, and I am here referring specifically to peanut butter and jelly sandwiches oozing grape jelly, and gloppy hamburgers stuffed with ketchup, relish and melted cheese.

The real American woman is willing to eat such food because she's a vibrant human being filled with joie de vivre and self-confidence. There is no languid picking at her food the European way. No. She likes a good meal. She enjoys keeping the child within alive and well. And she counters the unmentionable calories with runs, swims, yoga classes and skipping dinner for weeks at a time.

The true American woman will be seen eating that juicy burger. She will be spied dipping that peanut butter and jelly into milk, on a rainy day when she's feeling sorry for herself. And she will survive both these events in superlative health, and live to fit into her daughter's jeans.

Sometimes this gloppy food intake is just to make a

point. But more usually it's simply because she loves hamburgers and peanut butter and jelly sandwiches. Both are her go-to comfort food.

Certainly this is true for this American woman.

In a house with a white picket fence, there sits a pretty baby in her highchair. She reaches out and grabs the triangle cut of peanut butter and jelly sandwich so tightly between her pink fingers, a glittering globlet of grape jelly squeezes out of the side and slides down her chubby little arm. Startled she drops her triangle of peanut butter and jelly right into the cup of white milk sitting in front of her. It splashes as it lands, just a little bit. The baby startles again at the splash. She's delighted by the sound. She gazes for a moment at what she has wrought. The stuffed bread is floating in the cup as a milky stew grows around it. She reaches forward to retrieve her lunch from the cup and spots the globule of jelly clinging tenaciously to her arm. Her eyes widen once again. Because now she is caught between two equally wondrous quandaries—the wobbling, shining jelly on her arm, and the now soggy triangle of P&J drowning in that sea of milk, the jelly sending up tentacles of purple like a distress call from a squid.

And it is here, at this moment, the joy of peanut butter and jelly, the joy of dunking in a cup of milk, and the joy of jelly rolling down her arm is forever imprinted on her wide-open American soul as some of the finer pleasures in life.

The baby coos.

Her parents nod approvingly.

Personally, I like my peanut butter sandwiches slathered thickly with crunchy peanut butter and covered so thoroughly with grape jelly, the jelly drops out of the sides onto my hand before falling down into the glass of milk into which it has just been dipped.

I like my peanut butter and jelly sandwiches on multi grain bread. Honey wheat, to be precise. For that retro P&J sandwich, of course white bread would be the bread of choice. However, while basic and totally American in inspiration, my P&J sandwich is not retro. I don't use Welch's grape jelly either. I prefer France's Bonne Maman blackberry jelly, if I may be so bold.

There must be a glass of cold milk, into which I dip the sandwich for every bite. For this reason I cut my P&J sandwich into four squares. If I'm feeling a devil may care kind of freedom because after an incredible amount of hard work I'm hovering near my ideal weight, I make an extra half a sandwich which translates into a total of six squares. This necessitates a bigger glass of cold milk, but such are the trials of life in the fast lane.

The making of P&Js can be as creative as decorating the Christmas tree and as personal as one's very own belly button.

For instance, many times a P&J is not made with jelly at all.

First choice after jelly is honey. This version of a P&J is made by the organically conscious, but I throw in my vote too. The only problem is that the peanut butter and jelly made with honey does not go well dunked into milk. So for me, the P&J with honey is the one I bring on road trips, where the convenient glass of cold milk will not be readily available.

Mayonnaise goes perfectly with peanut butter. In fact, mayonnaise goes with absolutely anything, from cold roast beef to sliced apple. This is especially true if you spent time growing up in Brussels, Belgium like I did, and learned the good of mayonnaise.

So saying, a peanut butter and mayonnaise sandwich is popular. Especially among the young mothers set. Or, it was when I was a young mother. But it wasn't readily admitted. And what really wasn't admitted was the addition of potato chips to the peanut butter and mayonnaise sandwich. Potato chips were added for that crunch and that salt. A very tired friend of mine, who was the mother of four young sons, explained this to me one day with the same degree of shame and delight as though she were admitting to having an orgasmic affair on the side.

Finally, my most guilty P&J is the peanut butter and bacon sandwich. The bacon must still be dripping with grease. And instead of jelly, use honey. So that what you actually have is the sublime peanut butter, honey and bacon sandwich—

Which is, what can I say, to die for.

Now we spy another American baby. This baby is gazing solemnly at his parents. He suspects something very important is about to happen because they have the camera out. Both his parents are speaking in low, happy voices. They are in the kitchen. He is in his highchair, which he hates, and they have just cooked something. They seem excited about this food. They keep casting surreptitious glances in his direction. He's sucking his thumb, staring overtly back at them, wondering when the fistful of cheerios is going to dropped onto the tray of his highchair.

Finally they are done cooking. First they put their food on the big table. Then they put his food on his highchair tray. All the while they are cooing at him. He doesn't really understand them, much as he loves them. He discerns the cooing implies something very nice, like breastfeeding. But since he's stuck in his gloomy highchair, he knows that is not the reason for the cooing.

So yes, they have put a plate of something down in front of him. He doesn't take his thumb out of his mouth, but rather sucks a little more thoroughly as he beholds a round object that not only is steaming, it hasn't been cut up in little bites.

Mommy and Daddy lean in, encouraging him. Then they say a word he automatically understands.

"Hamburger," his all-American parents say. "This is a hamburger." They are beaming. They grab the camera and aim.

The great American hamburger. Every American in existence has heard of a hamburger. 99% of all Americans have eaten a hamburger.

Of all those Americans who have eaten a hamburger, 98% of them have very strong preferences as to how they like their hamburgers prepared. These preferences began to grow from that very first moment in the highchair.

Baby pops his thumb out of his mouth. In spite of himself, he's now curious. This is the biggest item his parents have ever placed in front of him to eat. And they seem even more excited about it than the first day they let him taste ice cream. Which didn't go well. Who knew babies had such a low tolerance for the ice cream. Certainly his parents didn't. They won't make that mistake with their second child, but this one, their first, just hasn't been so lucky. Like trying eggs too soon. Luckily Grandma was there that day or his

Mommy might have called an ambulance for the red flush he got immediately the egg hit his tongue. "Too soon, " said Grandma, the mother of six. "His system isn't ready."

So, hamburger.

He likes the way the word sounds. Could it be in the American DNA? Who likes a food just because they like the way the word sounds?

Baby does. He likes the word, and he likes the way the hamburger smells. He doesn't have words for the sultry aroma of hamburger grease and that touch of astringent ketchup, which is all his very first hamburger has on it. His parents aren't taking any chances with the strangeness of mustard or relish or even cheese. In fact Mommy called the pediatrician to make sure Baby could even attempt a bit of hamburger. "Go for it, " the pediatrician said heartily. Of course this was an American doctor who believed in the good of hamburgers. So Baby's mother told Daddy they were on for hamburgers. Which was fabulous news, because cooking all those mushy little extras for the baby was getting tiring and monotonous, and they were hoping it was about time he tried big boy food even though he was still breastfeeding.

This also spelled hope in the future for Daddy that barbecuing every week-end would soon be back in the cards.

Americans are opinionated about their hamburgers. For most, hamburgers consist of a meat pattie inside a bun, glopped up with a myriad of condiments. These are real people eating real hamburgers.

There are those Americans for whom the hamburger has lost favor as the perfect meal. These are those who are vegetarians, those who don't "do" red meat, those who have given up fun food for Lent, those who are vegans, raw foodies...

I don't have a problem with these people.

But there are those Americans who now, in the interest of restricting calories, remove the bun from their hamburger. I am appalled, and do not understand how they can look themselves in the mirror.

They persist in saying, rubbing their hands with glee, at a restaurant, in my kitchen, or even, dare I say, at some roadside stand, "I'll have a hamburger." Then they say, with a straight face, "Leave off the bun."

Leave off the bun?

Leave the bun off a hamburger? What one is left with, people, is a flat, miserly, gray, and totally ashamed little meat pattie. The bun is *not* a garnish. The bun isn't a nonfunctional part of the hamburger. The bun, my dear clueless American, the bun is what *makes* the naked pattie an *actual* hamburger.

Yes. I know it's all about weight control. Tell me about it.

But I just want you out there trying to be one of the guys by ordering a hamburger, a calorie ridden hamburger, and then slyly pulling the meat pattie out of the bun, and eating said meat...with a fork, may I die now...stop kidding yourself.

You have not just eaten a hamburger. A hamburger is eaten with the hands. Both hands. Both hands holding the luscious concoction aloft, grease and ketchup and mustard running down your elbows with each bite.

In-n-Out, which used to make THE BEST hamburgers in the whole wide world, now make one wrapped in lettuce. Lettuce?! Limp, watery, pale green, lettuce? I cried myself to sleep when the man I was with actually ordered his hamburger wrapped in lettuce. I called the whole thing off shortly thereafter.

The bunless hamburger?

Don't kid yourself, people.

The baby gazes down at the hamburger on his plate. Mommy has now cut it into fours. Admittedly, the ketchup does not squeeze out the sides. Nor is the meat so rare juice runs down onto the plate. Mommy is taking no chances with Baby's brand new digestive system. The juice running, the ketchup squeezing will come later. So will the raw onion, the swiss, the cheddar, the monterey jack or smoked gouda, the honey mustard or stone ground, the organic ketchup or homemade aioli, tomatoes, avocados, bacon, mushrooms, sprouts and lettuce.

Now the hamburger is doable, clutchable, eatable, if you are an eleven month old baby. He pops his thumb out of his mouth. He reaches for the hamburger. No qualms. His fingers easily clutch the soft hamburger bun. He brings the concoction—bun, meat ketchup and all—up to his mouth, where he takes a very thorough and adept bite. He chomps, and then looks up at his parents. His eyes light up as the juicy all-American meal hits his taste buds. Baby likes it! Mommy and Daddy, clutching each other's hands underneath the table, beam with happiness and pride at their first-born.

Baby chomps away, then drops the quarter burger down on his plate. It falls apart. He gazes at it stricken. But then, with all the concentration he puts towards pulling off his socks one at a time, he puts the bun back on top, grasps the reconstructed burger firmly between his fingers, and smiling straight up at his parents, he brings the whole thing back up to his mouth for his second bite of a real hamburger, bun and all.

The camera clicks.

When I ask myself again, what does it mean to be an American woman, the answer swims ashore like the first homo-sapiens emerging from the ocean. What it means to be an American woman is to know that at a really satisfying meal, one measly paper napkin won't be enough.

Lemonade Stand

The older I get, the farther afield my mind wanders. Given how long I've been alive, this makes for a lot of field in which to wander. Given how colorful and bountiful my fields are, well this makes for a creative, buoyant and colorful positive to aging.

My mind takes delight in this wandering mainly, because as I get older, I am better and better at keeping it in good fields. I try very hard to keep it away from wondering if my neighbor's habit of slamming her front door is the result of consuming too much sugar. I definitely stay away from convincing myself the world is going to end in my lifetime, or that a rogue wave in the middle of the Atlantic is going to be the way I go, or that Notre Dame might one day install elevators so that the woman of my age can once again visit the delights of the magnificent roof without being subjected to that harrowing climb by foot all the way up.

I avoid thinking about math or chemistry, mainly because I don't go to school anymore. I avoid berating myself for the fact I don't really understand where electricity comes from, no matter how many times it has been explained to me.

Things like that, see.

Today while driving home, my mind wondering if I

should get an app for French to improve, well, you know, my French, or should I maybe leap into the study of Italian because, well you know, I don't have anything else to do today, I had to jam on my brakes because the idiot in front of me suddenly had an attack of conscience and screeched to a stop in front of a grubby handmade lemonade stand on the corner of a congested suburban street.

Have you ever screeched to a halt in front of a home-made lemonade stand?

Have you? Have you ever actually drunk lemonade purchased at the lemonade stand with the sign that has the cents figure printed backwards?

So cute, right?

Wrong.

The home-made lemonade stand sitting right there on the corner of the intersection, looking adorably handmade is a totally manipulative fairytale that should be abolished.

I hate them and here's why.

First there are the vendors. These are really little kids who have only the vaguest idea what this is all about. I mean they sort of know about lemonade stands. They've certainly seen a tv show or film or even video game in which a cute little lemonade stand figures somewhere in the story line. But that's all they know. They don't know it's all Mommy's idea for keeping them occupied on a hot and endless summer day. It's also Mommy's idea because she too has seen those movies and tv shows featuring lemonade stands. The movie kids are always so adorable. Their Mommies too. She glows at the sight of the adorable fake Mommy who is so spotless and happy and in complete control in every situation involving her children. The advertising world is ruthless about destroying the real Mommies cracked egos. Because of the ruthless advertising world, the real Mommy sees herself as a failure in the child-rearing business.

But when she sees an image of the iconic lemonade stand, some weakly flickering flame of self-esteem flares, and she thinks "I can do that!"

The mystique of the cuteness of little children manning a lemonade stand in the summer heat is embedded in our American culture, but it completely eludes me. Mommies, a vulnerable lot if there ever was one, are moved to tears at the gentle notion of setting up the lemonade stand where their little darlings will have a fun-filled, and indeed ego-enhancing time, selling lemonade to kind and worthy strangers. Just like in bygone days when children actually had little red wagons and Lincoln Log sets.

I feel this ideal poses a threat to those of us not in the throes of Mommydom. There are those Mommies, who relentlessly twist the general public's arm to pay attention to their little darlings. And as a result, have morphed into the scum of the earth. I was that Mommy once, because of my wobbly psychological state. I remember the fury I felt if my shy little two year old gave a tentative wave in your direction, and you didn't fall on your face acknowledging him. So I understand from whence these Mommies come. But that doesn't mean I have to like it now, when my own sweet toddlers are all grown up and live by themselves and make their own snacks and all.

But even more annoying than the Mommies are the worthy strangers who abruptly stop their cars in the middle of an adrenaline-ridden, suburban intersection. These ferociously busy intersections are beehives of strained energy bearing all kinds of traffic. Mini-vans, huge SUVs, bicycles, nannies pushing carriages, skateboarders of all ages, dogs on leashes, dogs off leashes, loose children, and the few elderly folk who didn't move away from the child-ridden neighborhood in time. The worthy stranger slams on the brakes, leaps out to buy a paper cup of lemonade before she's even allowed a hint of second thoughts cloud her halo.

This enabler to the Mommies pays for and receives a paper cup half filled (because the kid can't hand over a full cup without spilling) with acrid lemonade because these Mommies don't realize that home-made lemonade requires a dumpster load of sugar to even begin to get it right…but that's another cooking lesson.

Then she stands there, Miss Do-Gooder, clutching a flimsy paper cup of pale yellow liquid which she is suddenly sure is *not* made from bottled water, because where would the profit be—

And…now what?

The do-gooder didn't think this one through, did she?

No, she didn't.

Well, what comes next is she actually has to drink the lemonade.

So the do-gooder takes a sip, and suddenly realizes she's about to consume 350 calories of sour lemonade, which will negate the 350 dessert calories she has diligently saved up to be able to consume, without gaining an ounce, that carrot cake she adores over at Java Wava Coffee. This almost sends the do-gooder over the bend because she's strict about sugar calories on top of being the kind of do-gooder who rips her afternoon schedule to shreds the minute she parked her gun metal gray Jeep (with dog in back). And so she experiences such a rush of rage it almost blows her head off. Because she finally realizes what she has actually done is sabotaged her day, for the insanely misguided need to be a do-gooder for this kid here. The kid who is, even now, looking around for his mother because this game isn't fun, he's scared of the lady who just bought the lemonade because she's giving off weird vibes, and he wants to go home.

Which serves her right. Because, having had to jam on my brakes for her to suddenly park her car right in front of me, is five minutes I'll never have back again...

Which brings me to pint-sized, door-to-door salesmen. I'm not totally heartless about the hopeful kid selling cookies or wrapping paper at the door—

Okay, I lie. I am totally heartless. I send them packing before they get one sentence out of their mouths. I coo my words of rejection, though. I coo softly and smile so sweetly at them. The cooing tone of voice tells them I am so sorry about the pain I know I'm causing. But it's for a good purpose, my kind, blue eyes tell them. It's to harden them. And they need to be hardened, by me, because their own mothers are too soft on them. So that here at my front door, where they have made the error of hope and knocked, I am doing them a big favor by telling them *NO* in capital letters.

Unless they are Girl Scouts selling Girl Scout cookies.

I always buy these in memory of my father. He loved Girl Scout cookies. Specifically the mint wafers and the peanut butter ones. And specifically because they only showed up once a year.

But where was Dad, back when I was eight years old and a reluctant Brownie myself? I was in Brownies because my mother and her best friend (who was the mother of my best friend) had volunteered to lead the troop, and Dad did not rescue me when the day came that I was supposed to get out there and sell the hell out of Girl Scout cookies.

I didn't know Brownies had that coda coming at the end of the year. It was fun until selling a dubious product door to door was introduced into the mix.

I watched my best friend sell boxes and boxes to her entire extended family without ever having to knock on a single front door. Since this was in Pittsfield, MA and my extended family lived in Louisville, KY, I didn't have that option. The door-to-door sale, even though I had no idea I would not have been the first pathetic person to knock on a stranger's door, was the most terrifying task I'd ever been set.

I made up my mind immediately. I was not going to do it. I was not going to knock on a single door. I knew I didn't care enough about Brownies to begin with. I cared about my Mom, though, which is why I'd done my time with good enough grace. But I had also been a New Kid that year, and by the time the door-to-door sales thing came around, I knew about rejection and knew I could face no more of it. I told my mother. She nodded and bought two boxes to see me through.

Like I said, where was Dad and his checkbook? Maybe this was before he discovered he loved Girl Scout cookies? He had three more daughters after me. Maybe that's when he found out he loved Girl Scout cookies, particularly the mint wafers and the peanut butter?

Anyway, the awards banquet (yes, even for Brownie troop participants) arrived, and the awards were given out for the most boxes sold. My mother may not have insisted I sell the cookies, but she sure as heck insisted I go to the banquet. There, I had to sit through each girl, having sold her eight million boxes of cookies to her family, receive her prize. I clapped. I was even relaxed because I knew my two boxes had to be way last, and therefore the powers-that-be would hand out three, maybe five prizes before everyone else got honorable mention, and my particular failure would be lost in the crowd of also-rans. But oh no. No way. The do-gooders back then had created an 'everybody wins' mandate. So that yes, every last Brownie got a prize.

Including me.

I was horrified. I couldn't believe it. I knew I had come in second to last. So it was a long wait for them to get to me. I was furious. Couldn't I have been allowed even a shred of dignity for being such a loser? No. I was called to the stage to receive my prize. My mother forced me to go up there and accept it. So I had to walk all the way up, wearing that brown uniform, sullen and graceless, praying I at least looked like I didn't care. The audience was quiet. No thrill of achievement here, so unlike the kid who'd sold three thousand boxes of mint thins to her adoring Grandma. No. Here was a quitter. A non-game player. A non-starter. A loner. Anti-social. An outcast in the making.

The smiling lady handed me my prize. I took it, muttered something about "I hate your guts…' Okay, I didn't. Then I slunk back to my table. And breathed a huge sigh of relief when the spotlight of failure moved from me to the pathetic crea-ture who came in dead last, and get this, she'd sold zero boxes of cookies. She looked sad enough about it, but who knows. Maybe her father and my father were friends, and it had never occurred to either one of them to help their sniveling, lay-about Brownie daughters with the cookie-selling nightmare—

Or maybe they were doing their best to see to it we didn't ever become door-to-door-saleswomen.

The prize, when I deigned to have a look, was not from a box of Cracker Jacks, as I had suspected. It was a solid comb in a plastic case. It wasn't bad, actually. And since it wasn't a bad prize, I did experience a moment of regret at what might have been had I tried even a little bit, sold maybe ten boxes, say, and maybe won a whole brush and comb set, in pink and glitter.

But just as my mother didn't sell my Girl Scout cookies for me, she also never set any of her six children up with a lemonade stand. Maybe because there were six of us, and my mother, having grown up on a farm, had a more pragmatic approach to parenting than the new Mommies.

But she'd obviously softened by the time her grand-children came along, because one summer she helped my five-year old son set up a traveling shell collection for sale in his red wagon. Yes. I got him a red wagon, and he loved it. My daughter loved hers too. She didn't like dolls though… you can't win them all.

The good news was he had actually collected these shells himself, out on the beach. This was made possible by the happy circumstance that his grandparents actually lived on the beach.

There were some nice ones in the collection. But mostly they were shell shards, broken, dull and completely lacking in beauty of any kind. He quite rightly wanted to keep the best ones for himself.

My mother did insist he wash the shells and shell piec-es first. Which begs the question—does the current day Mommy insist the kid make the actual lemonade?

So he had to wash his motley collection of shell bits and arrange them in his wagon. The bad news was, in terms of marketing know-how, since we were right on the beach, so was everyone else on my son's sales route…

When he finally returned from his travails, he had sold exactly no shells. And was completely shocked by this failure.

I was not pleased with my mother. I was that righteous Mommy who firmly believed in ego-enhancing escapades for my children. But my mother informed me her oldest grandson would live through the trauma. And then she took him off to the toy store to appease his little soul.

Solutions. My mother had them.

Although I don't remember being taken shopping for paper dolls after the Brownie cookie fiasco.

I saw a lemonade stand just the other day. Hence this particular field into which my mind wandered. I live in Southern California, but even so, the fact it's March gave me pause for thought. Seemed a little early in the year, didn't it, for lemonade stands? Aren't lemonade stands for the dog days of summer?

Then I realized it was spring break.

So then I wondered if the Mommies of today are getting more and more fragile and now can't even handle spring break without resorting to clogging up suburban intersections with lemonade stands.

I veered into thoughts of my bucolic youth, in the good ole days. Then I puttered though the good old days of my childrens' youth…

Then I realized I was the doddering old fool who thinks days of yore are the good old days, no matter history may say otherwise.

So I panicked and ate a quart of salt and caramel ice cream. A very modern flavor—

At least at the time of writing.

Losing Shirley Temple

Lagging lagging lagging. Down down down. It was hot and dusty, up there in the Swiss Alps. I was at a camp I hated. And I was on my way to a horseback riding lesson I hated.

I kicked at rocks in the dust as I went along. There were at least ten more days of this thirty-day stint up in the Alps. I was thirteen, and ten days were interminable.

Up ahead was a pharmacy with a small news kiosk outside. I passed by, glanced over at the newspapers ruffling in the hot breeze, and there blaring from the headlines of Le Figaro was

MARILYN MONROE EST MORT.

I skidded to a halt. Dust flew out behind me. I read the headline again. MARILYN MONROE EST MORT.

My world shook. Marilyn Monroe was dead? I couldn't wrap my brain around it at first. Dead was an ugly scary word. An unfair, vicious word. Something that happened to the very old. And the very unfortunate. Certainly not to a vivid blonde movie star who I knew was about the same age as my mother.

I knew about this Marilyn Monroe. Not much, but enough. She was that blonde American movie star who was maybe the most famous woman in the world, and even though I was hazy on the details, I knew her death was all wrong. I knew she was too young to die. I could sense that something had gone terribly wrong for Marilyn Monroe. Seeing the headlines in French made it even worse for me. They sounded all wrong, too. This was about an American. She wasn't theirs. She was ours.

Sudden tears rolled down my cheeks. All that should have been sunny and light in my world went even darker. The nasty kids I had to hang silently around. And now this calamity from America. For I knew it was a calamity. The newspapers wouldn't have blared it otherwise. MARILYN MONROE EST MORT.

I turned right around and walked back to where we would all meet later to catch the cable cars back up to the camp itself. I picked a bench in the shade, and waited.

MARILYN MONROE EST MORT.

I never went back to another horseback riding lesson. They couldn't make me. And for some reason they didn't.

Where was I when the first man stood on the moon? I was in Laguna Beach, CA, and I didn't know my best friend would be killed in a car accident a week later. When she was killed my first confused thought was since she'd seen a man on the moon it would help her adjust to her new reality. Then I cried for the nine months, until she came to me in a dream, hugged me and told me goodbye. I woke up and began to heal.

Where was I when Nadia Comeneche scored that first perfect ten in an Olympics? I was in the tv room of my parents' house in Chicago, IL. A ten! And they said it couldn't be done!

Where was I when Charles Manson and his crew killed Sharon Tate and everyone else that hideous night? My husband and I were lying in bed of our first apartment one night after the murders, before anyone had been caught, and gunfire suddenly erupted close by. At least that's what we thought is was. It was three am. We looked at each other, sudden terror taking hold. We got out of bed, threw on some clothes, leapt into my husband's ancient little Porsche and drove off. Ten hours later we arrived in Lake Tahoe, too young to gamble, almost too young to get a motel room for the night. The engine of the Porsche blew up on the way home, the Sierra Nevadas simply being too much for it. But we had managed to shake the grip of the weird madness of the Manson murders.

Where was I when Obama, the first black president of the USA, was elected? I was in Paris.

Where was I when I voted for him? In Paris, where I voted by absentee ballot. I waited in the post office line, none too sure I was in the right line. And sure enough, when I finally reached the front of the line, the young man behind the counter saw I needed to mail a large envelope and sadly, aware of my wait, directed me to another line and started to turn away. But I was desperate. I wanted to make sure I got my absentee ballot in on time. It had taken a circuitous route to get to me in Paris in the first place. So I blurted out "S'il vous plait, monsieur. C'est mon voting ballot pour Barak Obama."

The young man stopped in his tracks. He turned back around. "Ah," he said. "Donnez-moi." And he stamped the envelope himself.

"Par Avion?" I said, still worried.

"Bien sur, Madame," he said, and smiled that beautiful smile Parisians have when they decide to use it. "La plus vite. Pour votre Barak Obama."

Where was I when President Kennedy was shot? I was twelve and living in Belgium.

And Jacqueline Kennedy? Where was I when she died?

When Jackie Kennedy died my mother and I were together. She was visiting from Chicago. We were sitting in the kitchen of my Baltimore house having coffee. Both babies were down for their naps. The kitchen floor was literally covered with their toys, with their enthusiasm for life. I'd stood up to get the toasted English muffins and avocados and butter, and from behind me my mother, finally taking a first glance at the morning paper, said quietly, "Jackie Kennedy died." I swung around, and our eyes met with a sudden mutual sorrow, the role this beautiful woman had played in the world's lives, and now, just like that, she was gone.

We were living in Brussels, Belgium when President Kennedy was assassinated all those years ago, and I remember my outraged shock that someone had actually killed that amazing man. And the blood all over Jackie Kennedy's cherry colored suit. And Lyndon Johnson taking the oath in that jet, the shock of the whole moment playing on everyone's faces even as they all strove for calm.

And later, our next door neighbors, a Belgian Duke and Duchess whom we'd never seen, came over, on foot, to knock on our front door, where they, elderly and elegant, and with immense dignity in spite of their tears, stood weeping, telling my parents how very very sorry they were for our country's horrendous loss, and not only our loss, but the world's loss.

And how at his work, my father's Belgian employees came one by one to offer their regrets for his terrible loss, and for the terrible loss for his country. In French and Flemish.

And how our school, the International School of Brussels

closed for two days, and the church bells tolled, all over, there in Brussels, Belgium, so far away from Dallas, Texas and Washington DC.

And how my four-year old sister needed an emergency appendectomy the day Jack Ruby was shot. The hospital called their head surgeon out of a formal dinner to operate on the little daughter of Americans who had just lost their president. He flew in the door, still dressed in full tails. And how he performed the surgery so skillfully, my sister's scar barely shows. This when an appendectomy scar was often long and jagged.

And how beautiful Jackie Kennedy had looked all through those horrendous days, and how young she was, I realize now. How very young, and John-John saluting and Caroline hanging her head, holding her mother's hand—

"She was an elegant woman," said my mother, in my kitchen in Baltimore, as I put the toasted muffins on the table. "She always handled herself beautifully," said my mother, who never had anything good to say about celebrity.

Where was I when Robert Kennedy was shot? Los Angeles. Stuck in the traffic being held up by the airport to make way for his entourage, and I was pissed because I needed to get back to school in Palos Verdes to study for my French final. I got back to the dorm, and later on heard Robert Kennedy had been shot. I threw my French text book at the wall. Rage. Simple rage. I didn't study anymore for the exam, and passed it anyway.

Where was I when John Lennon was shot, and Janis Joplin died of an overdose and Brian Keith, and Jimi Hendrix too. By the time the drug overdoses of my generation's rock

stars and movie stars too, came along, I was a hardened pur-
veyor of death by excess. I'd feel such anger at my heros
for being such fools, that I began sniffing out drug abusers
and keeping them off my roster of favorites. My daughter
wasn't knowledgeable enough yet, when years later her Kurt
Cobain committed suicide.

Where was I when I first heard that planes had crashed
into the World Trade Center? I was at an AA meeting in
Laguna Beach. Which was a very good place to be because
one of our most loved old timers, who had grown up in San
Francisco, told us how her best friend, who was Japanese
American, had been placed put in an internment camp for
Japanese American's immediately following Pearl Harbor.
She said it was the most shocking thing that had happened to
her up until then. She was twelve, as was her friend. She insisted we remember that we must not judge an entire people
by the acts of a few.

And Elvis Presley?

My brothers and sisters and I were testy and irritable and
fighting with each other on a rainy day in Balboa, California
in the middle of the summer. We were all pissed off it was
raining, raining raining in August, who knew why. It was obviously some ridiculous fluke of weather that summer. It had
been overcast for the past few weeks and our hard earned
tans were fading before our very eyes just as we were about
to go back to Chicago, where instead of being able to strut
about with sexy tans, we were about to fade into the wood-
work, enduring taunts from our Midwest friends about the
frailty of the Californian sun. And now Mother Nature had
finally even gone so far as to rain in Southern California in
August.

The tourists were down because of the rain, so we sulkily

agreed to take the ferry across to Balboa Island for the fun of it, to get wherever it was we were going. We were right in the middle of the channel, on the ferry, yacking and bickering, when suddenly the music on the radio stopped and a voice said "Elvis Presley is dead."

The car went silent. Even my oldest brother. "This is a joke," said my younger brother, after a moment. But no. The voice of the radio continued on in a quiet and excited fashion about where Elvis been found, how he'd been found, what he had been wearing when he was found, the state of his health in general.

Those were the days when drug overdoses were only hinted out, but we knew. We were cool young people. We knew why that wreck of a man had died. And we were not okay with it. We were not okay with Elvis Presley suddenly leaving this earth, forever. My brother snapped the radio off.

"I don't believe it," said my sister-in-law, into the sudden silence.

The ferry reached the other side. Quiet now with confused shock, we drove slowly up off the ferry, and quietly through the rain sodden streets of quaint Balboa Island.

Where were we when amazing happiness strikes?

I was in Newport Beach when I found out I was pregnant with my first baby. We'd been trying for two years, and I had begun to give up hope.

I was in Paris when Barak Obama was elected, and for the first time ever, my newspaper guy at my local kiosk smiled at me when I pointed to the headlines blaring Obama's triumph. "At last," he said. "Your country does something good." I swear for the rest of the trip people smiled at me, recognizing the American who was from the country that had the smarts to elect such a man as Obama as president. The world hadn't believed we had the guts to do it.

I was standing down at the end of my driveway in Baltimore, MD, by the mailbox, when I got my first publishing acceptance. There is sat, in the middle of the bills, an envelope from the literary journal Epoch. My heart sank. So far these had always been rejections. But this envelope was longer, bigger. Or was that just my imagination. I opened it right there, one of my cats winding in and out of my feet. "We are happy to tell you that your story "Way Station" has been accepted for publication..." Stardust appeared!

My mother won a car when we were living in Belgium. She said she couldn't believe it. She'd never won anything before. And now? A car! But when she tried to call Dad, he was in a meeting. Her closest friends were not answering their phones.

I was in school, and suddenly the principal's assistant appeared at the door of my classroom and gestured over to my teacher. They both looked at me. I was beckoned to follow the assistant to the principal's office. The principal was standing at his desk. He handed me a phone. I barely noticed he was smiling. I took the phone. "Hello," I whispered.

"Ruthie, I won a car!!! It's a Fiat. Your father was busy. My friends aren't home. I had to tell someone! I hope I didn't get you out of anything. *I won a car!*" My mother's voice was a pitch higher. Her Southern drawl in full flower. She was as delighted as I'd ever seen her. I was a puberty stricken twelve year old. But I could hear it, and I'll never forget her amazed and unbridled joy.

The death of Shirley Temple hit me in my tender spot. My tender spot, it turns out, is soft memories of my childhood. Usually they are about when I lived in Pittsfield, Massachusetts. In the heart of the Berkshire Mountains. On Dawes Avenue. When I was eight to eleven.

This is where I first heard of Shirley Temple. I don't know if it was a grainy clip of her dancing and singing, or a collage of photographs of her unbearably charming visage. Or those curls. Or that thirties wardrobe of hers. I loved every dressing table ever concocted by the Hollywood system for their leading ladies, and then they gave the very same thing to the most adorable child in the world, Shirley Temple.

So there she was, in my life forever.

When I was eleven, we moved across the country to Oakland CA. I had to leave my BFF Andi McCall behind. It was heart rending. But like a gift from my worried guardian angel, it turned out there was a show on tv on Sunday afternoons that played Shirley Temple movies.

My mother found the show. There was a large bay alcove and bay window on the second floor of our house, quite open to the rest of the floor. This is where our television was, and every Sunday, from 3:00 to 4:30, one of these angelic gems aired. I was glued to the window seat. No one bothered me, including my younger brother, or any of the little sisters. It was only later I realized my mother must have kept everyone out of the way, because I only recall I was blissfully alone, getting my Shirley Temple fix, in a house filled with five other children,

Her old movies were hard to come by, and when we moved to Brussels, Belgium the next year, our regular television shows were gone for the duration. So my parents sought out and found a beautiful picture book of Shirley's films, with the abridged story accompanying several photos from each movie. There was Rebecca of Sunnybrook Farm,

Heidi, Captain January, The Littlest Rebel and Susannah of the Mounties. I was in heaven.

Life goes on, and I've never outgrown Shirley Temple. She retains her part in my heart that represented purity with sass, luxury with a boldness that got her in and out of trouble. The fact the child entertainer grew up to become a successful woman in so many ways, just adds to her aura.

And now she has died. For me, the world is missing an angel.

The day John Lennon was murdered I had a nine month old baby and a two year old. I was playing housewife/ Mommy, and I was having two friends over for lunch—also with babies. When they walked in the door, carrying babies (one was a six week old infant with an unhappy three year old sister...) diaper bags, various important toys, teething rings and pacifiers, for some reason, neither of them shared my shock and sorrow.

I couldn't believe it. They didn't care that John Lennon had been murdered? Killed with a gun. I put a bib around my daughter's neck. I appeased my two year old son about I don't know what. The infant was fed every second, much to the distress of her older sister. Toys got strewn. We ate something. Probably peanut and butter and jelly sandwiches just to keep things simple, and maybe to encourage the older babies to do the same thing as us Mommies, instead of the same thing as the under-nine-month old crowd.

Maybe that's why my friends were underwhelmed by the loss of John Lennon. Not only the loss but the method in which he was dispatched from this world.

Maybe because we all could remember exactly where we had been when JFK was assassinated. The first of the violent or drug related deaths to proliferate during the sixties. Let alone the personal violence the Vietnam War had laid at our door, affecting our boyfriends or very young husbands. We were broken in, so to speak, to the fact of violent and pointless death, so often happening to our current icons. Maybe that is why their babies rang larger for my friends that day John Lennon was killed.

But not to me. That day was bleak. In fact, it actually was a bleak day, grey and cold, in December, in Baltimore, MD. Even my kitchen, redolent in babies and diapers and powder and peanut butter and jelly, seemed bleak to me. A light had gone out. My favorite Beatle. Something from my youth had flickered and was over before I was ready.

So that today, the day Shirley Temple died, that part of me that has Shirley Temple in my heart, a part of my heart that first let her in when I was nine years old, has gone out.

It will subside, of course.

But it aches a bit. That's all. It aches.

My Mother's Death

One Sunday morning in May, surrounded by her husband of fifty-nine years and her six children, in her home in her own bed, my mother died.

After everyone but my sisters had left the room, I held her in my arms, her head lolling on my chest. I was thinking how heavy her head was, how very heavy. How ineffably vulnerable. My mother. I was holding my mother, who was dead, in my arms. I was holding her, caring for her now at this amazing moment of her death, when it had been she who had held me at the amazing moment of my birth.

I thought also of two tiny heads lolling on my chest, so much lighter, but impacting so heavily—the heads of my newborn infants. In that case I was seeing them into this life. I was starting them on their way. I was listening to the sound of their new breath with awe. Feeling their tiny chests move.

Now, there was no breath coming from my mother. Not a sound. No rising up and down of her chest. Now I was seeing my mother out of this life.

Her head was lying on my chest because my sisters and I were dressing her before she was to be taken to the mortuary. We had decided what we were going to put on her. We had taken off her pajamas. Soft flannel because she had been so delicate, so easily hurt, by the time she died.

But I was insisting we put a bra on her. My sisters, careful with me, as we were all being careful with each other, told me no, arguing it made absolutely no sense to do that. But I wouldn't let it go. I wanted a bra on her. It didn't seem right—

"Her bras are too big," said one of my sisters, finally. I am the oldest sister. I should have known better. I should have be keeping calm for them. She looked at me almost desperately. I was making it worse. I was pointing up the madness. Our beloved mother had actually died. Please please please shut up about the pointless bra—

"Okay," I whispered. My head tried to clear.

It was turning out to be harder to dress our mother than we had thought. A dead body is a dead weight. Even though my mother was so light by the time she died.

Or was it because our hearts were too broken to be fully capable.

Her head lolled on my chest, and then in my arms as we moved her here and there, rolling her as needed from side to side, dressing her. As I was the only one of us who'd had children, and my expertise having been honed while dressing rigid, angry two year olds, I was able to direct the arms being pulled into sleeves, just so. Her legs being pulled into pants by first rolling the pant leg up as much as possible. All the while my mother's body was a rag doll, so unlike anything she had been in real life.

But this *was* real life. Mom, our very own Mom, had just died. "Here, hold her arm like this. Now ease her head through here. Now roll her to the left," I said. Our strong mother. The mother who'd dressed us. Now we were dressing her, fifteen minutes after her death.

We put her in one of her beautiful pants and jackets,

easy, elegant, simple. We decided against jewelry, although a different sister had to be convinced of this. We brushed her hair. She had beautiful thick hair which still sprang from her scalp, only slightly ruined by her final illness. We decided against shoes. "They'll hurt her feet," said another one of us. "Like the bra would have—"

Then we smoothed the bedclothes under her, and laid one of her favorite coverlets over her up to her chest. We put her hands together on her chest. We'd seen in movies how to do this. And then we straightened up the bedroom, removing all sick room paraphernalia. We pushed aside the curtains. We opened the windows. Sunlight entered gently, honoring the beautiful but lifeless body who, as we could still barely comprehend, was our very own mother.

We were grey. We were ghosts in our own lives. Our mother had actually just left this world. Had left us.

Then we opened the bedroom door. The rest of the family was hovering, mute with dawning grief. Then one at a time, everyone had their turn to come and sit quietly with Mom and tell her whatever was in their broken hearts.

Thank heaven for shock at such moments. The mundane issues become refuge. "We should eat," my sister-in-law said a bit later. And within fifteen minutes a large meal of leftovers was set out on the dining room table, and we all straggled together and tried to eat, as our mother lay back in her bedroom, someone with her every moment, until we could bear to call the mortuary to come and take her away.

There were a lot of us there. My older brother. My younger brother and his wife and their son. My son, who is the same age as theirs, twenty-five years old. Two of my younger sisters, and their partners. My husband.

And then there was my father. Too stunned to speak.

It had been six weeks of watching, helping, learning how to do it, learning how to care for a mortally ill person. Her hospital bed had been set up in the living room. She spent the day there, but then went back to her room with Dad for the night. We all rotated helping, but I moved in with Dad, so that I was there every day and night. Except Saturday nights, when I went back home to my husband for the night, and where my cats were quiet with worry, and indeed the youngest one so confused, I started bringing her back to the beach house with me. Seeing Mom flinch the day my little Siamese almost jumped up on the bed to be with her hit me more that her delicate appearance, how oh so terribly fragile she had become. My sturdy mother who would have loved to have a cat leap up on her anytime.

Hospice was incredible. Not what I thought it would be exactly. I thought they would move in. But no. They sent people over for baths, massages and so on. But we were to deal with the daily care. The pill regime, the enemas, because even though her body was dying, it also was still weakly functioning. My sister and I took turns with the enemas. My mother held on to her dignity and submitted. My sister always got better results.

But I could get her to eat more, even though hospice gently told me it simply didn't matter what she ate. Let her have whatever she wanted.

She had two bowls of strawberry ice cream one time. Another time, my plate of huevoes rancheros looked so good to her she asked for a plate of her own. I made it. She ate it all. And somewhere in all our hearts that night, when we went to bed, we allowed ourselves a breath of hope. Of hope this was all a bad dream, and our strong Mom would get up out of her bed, made healthy and whole by those huevos rancheros.

Our house was directly on the beach. She loved the pelicans that flew up and down the Pacific coast. They flew down south in the morning, and came back late in the afternoon. I never actually knew what their habits were, but this daily fly-by was lovely, and my mother looked forward to it.

I was standing out on the front deck, just after she died. The pelicans were flying by. Then quite suddenly and deliberately, four of them peeled away from the pod and flew right over the roof of the house, right over the bedroom where she lay. Their approach was swift and sure. They've caught her soul, I thought, so strong was their flight. Then they flew back to join their own. I exhaled and clutched the railing.

The sun was watery that day, May 19, 2002. The water was pale. It was a Sunday. I had been sleeping at home with my husband when the phone rang at 3:30 am. "Your mother is dying," my father gasped into the phone.

My husband never drove fast on the freeways. He was from Baltimore, and although he tore around the city streets, he drove like an aging coot on the freeways. But not that morning. He sped over to the beach house. And I ran into the house.

It was six more hours before my mother died. I lay on the bed next to her and fell asleep holding my mother's hand. Or was she holding mine?

My older brother called my younger brother. He wasn't at home but his wife, my sister-in-law, a nurse, listened to my brother say that Mom was worse and things seemed to be happening, but he didn't think they needed to rush up from

San Diego just yet. When they hung up, my sister-in-law immediately called my brother and said "Now. We have to get up there now."

I remember that my mother waited to take her last breath until they arrived. But my brother says no. He says that he was hastening up to the house, and all of a sudden he was completely enveloped in a huge, overpowering warmth of love, and he knew it was Mom, and that she had died. They rushed into the bedroom, red faced but trying for calm, after the two hour drive.

The rest of us were sprawled all over the bed with her. Her breath had gotten more sharp. Longer intervals in between each one. Almost like she'd forgotten she was supposed to breath when there would suddenly be another sharp inhale. The intervals between breaths became longer and longer until finally my older brother called out, his voice sounding like a little boy, "Thank you, Mom."

Then she died.

Our perfect mother died, right in front of our disbelieving eyes.

The next day my daughter and I were standing at water's edge. It was a quiet day. The waves were lapping. And then out of somewhere, one perfect red rose bud washed right up to our feet.

"Meemaw," said my daughter, and burst into tears.

Even after hospice became involved, my mother never talked about her death. But she did want to see where she was to be buried. My father and sister Barbara had picked out the spot. It was a double spot, with Dad's place right there too. We drove over, and although very fragile, Mom wanted to get out of the car and feel the air. There were large trees. It was a pretty day, with a gentle breeze. It seemed to put its best foot forward. To ease her fears. We are a gentle place, it whispered to her. We are welcoming.

"This is nice, she said softly. "Don't you think?" she looked at me.

"Oh yes, Mom. Very nice," I said. Yes, it was nice. It was calm.

On the way home she talked about her funeral a bit. "No open casket," she said. "And that new suit you bought last week, Jim," she said to my father, "It was for my funeral, wasn't it."

Dad sputtered. "No!"

One time later, she called me over to her bed and told me she had just had a dream in which I had bought a dotted Swiss dress. She wanted to know if it was for her funeral. I reared back in mock horror, and told her I would never buy dotted Swiss anything. That she had had her chance putting me in all that dotted Swiss when I was growing up. And that furthermore, I hadn't bought any dress for any funeral.

My mother never talked about her death. One sister asked her if she had any last words for her. My mother gazed at her and said "No."

She did say the only death she had ever seen was the death of Dad's grandmother, Carrie. "It was gentle," she said. "She was in her own bed, and all the family was gathered around. I would like to die like that."

She died exactly like that.

It was the longest six weeks in the world, and the shortest in my memory.

My father still berates himself for the time she woke up

and told him he was to go to the baseball game with every-one, and not stay home with her. And he tried to tell her she was just dreaming and there was no baseball game. "I should have said okay, Margaret. I'll go to the baseball game with everyone. Why didn't I just say that?"

I kept trying to feed her. Healthy food. Even when she barely wanted to eat. Even when she maybe wanted a bit of ice cream. Even when the hospice people had told me she was to eat whatever she wanted. Or not eat at all. Because at this point, food was not helping her body at all. This was a concept I could barely take in. That her ill body, her dy-ing body was no longer using food as nutrition in the way a healthy one would. Not in the way I was using them—to help her get better.

She was not getting better. She was dying.

She was letting go. Not consciously. But as her body shut down, so did her enthusiasm, her sense of humor, her curios-ity, her stamina and energy. Her spirit quietly let down too. Her life faded out. Right before our incredulous eyes.

Oh she was so gracious. Right to the end. A beautiful and gracious Southern woman. Always said thank you. Always flashed that lovely Southern smile. Never choked on a single pill. Never yelled or got angry.

She had dreams in her last weeks of those closest to her who had died. Her mother and her sister. She dreamed a priest came, and asked her to take a walk with him, "And I did," she said, "Even though I left your father behind."

And then that phone call at 3:30 am.

And the high speed drive over to her.

And then my sisters and I were dressing her still warm, lifeless body. And I was thinking, I am holding my dead mother just like I held my new born babies, just like she held me, just like she held my two sister helping me, just like she'd held all six of her children when we were born.

Her head was so heavy. So incredibly heavy.

I have been permanently cast adrift. The mother who bore me into this world has left it. I will never see her again. Some times the black hole of that the pitiless fact sweeps over me and sucks me down so sharply I can't breathe. Sometimes out of nowhere, I burst into wracking, gasping sobs.

My daughter said to me one time, "I am so glad it wasn't you, Mom. I don't know what I would do if I lost you."

That helped. It brought me back to my other role, that of being a mother myself.

That I am a mother helps right my world when I am stunned all over again, by the irrevocable and completely unacceptable fact that my very own precious mother has died and is gone from me here on this earth, for the rest of my life.

Am I Wise Yet?

This seemed like a simple question when I first posed it to myself.

The answer was yes. Of course I am. By virtue of the fact I've lived a long time and I've raised children who survived the process.

But really? That made me wise?

And what does wisdom even mean?

What does wise mean to me today? Facing the last trimester of my life.

Wise. You can have it. Now go away and leave me alone...

No?

Okay. My own wisdom, such that I may have is that I've learned how to keep myself sane, and even happy, when the chips are down.

For instance, I've learned how to keep myself sane and happy when I am alone and afraid. Or when my mother was dying, or when it seemed like I was going to lose my son to drug addiction, or when my husband's business crashed.

Or when sciatica shows up once again.

On a lesser level, my wisdom shows up when I am in

everyday strife. For instance when I'm in a foreign country and have found myself in the wrong park just after dark, and I see hostile faces beginning to appear in the shadows, and I realize with a silent shout of alarm that I had better get the out fast. So I leave walking confidently, even while my armpits are soaked.

What I mean is I no longer waste one minute spiraling downward into negative thinking. I either spring into action. Or I sit still and figure it out.

"Conventional wisdom" The very phrase leads me to believe the word wisdom is used incautiously. That there is nothing conventional about wisdom.

Wisdom is time and the ages coming to bear on one's own personal space, one's own little spot on this earth.

Wisdom is white light crying out to be heard, but in the gentlest form.

Wisdom is the quiet after a loud day, a quiet in which we can hear the heart beat we haven't thought about all day.

Wisdom is the sound of our mind speaking quietly and with love.

I believe wisdom is there for anyone calm enough to take a moment and listen.

Listen quietly, though.

Very quietly.

Wisdom doesn't shout.

Notes
for
Fabulous Flying Forward

In no particular order:

Because we no longer have to do things in order, do we?

Travel *by yourself* somewhere glorious, edgy or glamorous. Like Paris, London or Iceland, or even the next state over from yours. Hong Kong or Rio de Janero if that's your cup of tea. Katmandu or Mont Blanc. New Orleans. Chicago. Now there's a fabulous city. Stay for a month in an apartment so that you must deal with daily life in a foreign language. Magic will happen. Always. And when you get home, you will be soaring. Your self-confidence will know no bounds. Your soul will be resting easy, so beautifully easy. Because you will have changed in some subliminal way.

Exercise. More than ever. Muscles go so fast, especially after sixty. I used to have six weeks of sitting on my ass before muscles began to fall apart. Now it's a week. If I'm lucky. Pilates, yoga, hiking, jogging, ball room dancing, mountain climbing, horseback riding, the gym, boxing, marathons, Zumba, power walking. Find something. Do it. Forever.

Maintain relationships with your friends. Have a lot of them. From as many different groups as you can realistically keep up with. Have friends from different age groups and ethnic groups. Never have just one group.

Be a member of a community. Church, AA, hiking club, chess club, investment club. Nurture your community which will in turn nurture you.

Make alone time a priority if you live surrounded by people and can't hear yourself breathe. Make getting out socially a priority if you live alone and the sound of your breathing is too loud. I've lived both ways…I do both.

Keep your lingerie updated. Single or married. Do it now. Do not wait until you are on the verge of your first love affair in too long time (like I did), to notice your underwear has gone gray and tattered. You will be shocked at what it cost to update (like I was).

In a rut? Think outside the box. Consider the impossible, pointless or ridiculous Whatever your version of this is:

Consider a month in Key West.

Christmas lights in the back yard, all year round.

Consider getting three kittens, maybe four.

Consider going blond or redheaded.

Consider being the one who leaves her phone on during the movie and who answers it during a love scene.

Consider arguing with the teenaged traffic cop.

Consider buying a huge house instead of downsizing.

Consider getting a cleaning person even if you live in a 850 square foot apartment. Consider having her/him come more often if living in a larger place.

Get sexy sheets for the bedroom. Maybe turquoise or deep purple. Get rid of the farmhouse look that seemed so appealing when you first moved in (note to self).

Call the accountant before she calls you to discuss taxes. Argue with your doctor. Double check his info with your pharmacist.

Ignore weather reports before you get in the car to drive cross-country.

Ignore your rising concerns about rogue waves, and sign up for the ocean cruise of your dreams. Go to a therapist to find out why you are suddenly afraid of rogue waves (note to self).

Watch all the TV you want. TV is amazingly good these days.

Demand your grown children respond to your texts on the same day you send them. Inform them if they don't, you'll start telephoning them again. Tell them to be grateful you even like to text and are willing to be satisfied with happy emojis instead of hearing their voices.

Say no to the gala event at which you know you will be bored out of your mind, and will cost you big bucks. The only reason you ever agree to these things is because you love deciding on the outfit. Buy the outfit anyway.

Do not shuffle your feet when you walk, especially while wearing flip flops.

Do not lean on your shopping cart in the grocery store or Costco...unless you're ninety-three...and maybe not even then.

Do not eat snacks at midnight. Wait until breakfast and eat them then.

Take the road of righteous good behavior, lose the ego when it's a good idea, don't bang on closed doors, breathe deeply, smile at your beautiful self in the mirror every day... several times if necessary, love your children and pets and partners more than anything in the world, say please and thank you—

And thou shalt be the prism in the sun, the depth in the ocean, the kid at the birthday party, and Greta Garbo at her dressing table.

Okay?

Getting older is here.

Fly with it.

Yes it takes guts.

And you have them.

Because baby, you are the boss of you.

Also by
RUTH YUNKER

Me, Myself and Paris
*One Toe Under the Eiffel Tower,
The Other In the Grocery Store*

Paris
*I've Grown Accustomed To
Your Ways.*

Me, Myself and Paris
One Toe Under the Eiffel Tower, The Other In the Grocery Store

Me, Myself & Paris is author Ruth Yunker's droll pastiche of her days, free and unaccompanied, in Paris. Three years in a row she rents an apartment, stays for six weeks, and takes on Paris, half resident, half visitor. She is a short attention span tourist, a wide-eyed voyeur, and irreverence saves the day when the chips are down. Her stories are about bonhomie and savoir-faire, American style, while treading the hallowed and slippery cobblestones of Paris.

It's about every day errands, and sorties into dutiful sightseeing. It's about run-ins with grocery store cashiers and metro ticket agents. It's about desperately trying to speak French. It's about attempting to emulate the chic, windblown Parisian woman wearing no lipstick, while Ruth wouldn't be caught bare lipped outside the boudoir.

She conquers the metro, no mean feat for a Californian glued to a car. She hears ghosts in cathedrals, and smells bread toasting every morning across the courtyard. She learns to make correct change without her reading glasses. Comes to understand that direct eye contact is a flagrant disregard of manners, even when she most needs a hug.

Me, Myself & Paris is what Paris looks like, feels like, smells like, tastes like, to an American woman, free and unfettered, sense of humor and bonhomie alive and well, alone and loving it, in the most beautiful and temperamental city in the world.

Paris
I've Grown Accustomed To Your Ways.

Paris I've Grown Accustomed To Your Ways continues the saga begun in Me, Myself and Paris, humorist and writer Ruth Yunker's account of her forays into life in Paris, part time tourist, part time resident. In Paris, I've Grown Accustomed To Your Ways the training wheels have come off. Ms. Yunker negotiates the exquisitely charming, but impossibly exacting, City of Light with a new sense of ease, and an increasing sense of feeling right at home. She revels in the amber warmth of Angelina's chocolate Eden on a cold November day. She zeroes in on, after six visits, her favorite arrondissement in which to rent her apartment...the fifteenth, just so you know! She shops in Montmartre with aplomb, and still does not climb up to the top of the Eiffel Tower. She sees passionate love in unexpected places out on the streets of Paris. She watches cowboys riding the metros, and considers the sweet life of a lemon as it rolls out of her apartment door. A little boy in St. Sulpice wins her heart. The concierge at the apartment on rue Vaneau does not. She discovers there are rules for finishing one's plate in restaurants. But there are no rules for which pain rustique will make the very best toast every morning. In Paris, I've Grown Accustomed To Your Ways, Ruth Yunker delves deeply to discover what makes the heart of Paris sing, and emerges more in love than ever.

CPSIA information can be obtained
at www.ICGtesting.com
Printed in the USA
LVOW03s1527210318

570659LV00001B/192/P